Endorsements

The extraordinary story o[...] fraudster and conman who fooled central banks, elite universities, major companies and scores of individual business leaders is in itself captivating and astounding, but he also plied a series of smart sophisticated women with seductive invitations, extravagant gifts and lashings of Yeats…

Anne Summers AO, author of *Unfettered and Alive*, and *Damned Whores and God's Police*.

Raw and honest…A sadly too common tale of how ego and hubris wreak harm, but equally a testament that the only way to break these cycles is to tell the truth.

Amy Richards, Producer of the Emmy-nominated *Woman* (Viceland) and author of *We Are Makers*.

Vivid and transparent. Deft. I was absolutely hooked from the first paragraph, and the creeping sense that something was amiss was masterful. The fundamental power is the unflinching basis in truth.

Professor Joanna Benjamin (Emeritus Professor of Law, The London School of Economics).

A gripping and haunting account of trust betrayed that you won't be able to put down – a story of dreams, reality, and the wide gap between the two that too often engulfs us all.

Amanda L. Tyler, co-author with Ruth Bader Ginsburg on *Justice, Justice Thou Shalt Pursue*.

This brave fable is an intimate portrait of a relationship destroyed by betrayal, as well as a reflection on our troubled time's preoccupation with breaches of the public trust. The author leads us thus to the moral of the story: that trust is both fragile and essential and must somehow be helped to flourish; that every betrayal of trust, public or private, ultimately harms each of us and diminishes our ability to live together with open hearts.

Vicki Laveau-Harvie, author of 2019 Stella Prize-winning memoir *The Erratics*.

Trust

Jeanne Ryckmans

Jeanne Ryckmans has worked for two decades in
Australian publishing. Now a literary agent, she
was formerly senior publisher at Random House
and HarperCollins Australia. Prior to this she
worked in arts television in France and Australia
as presenter, producer and documentary director
and was features editor at *ELLE* Magazine and
books editor for *Vogue* Australia. She is the
author of two previous books.

Jeanne Ryckmans

Trust

A fractured fable

First published in Australia in 2023
by Upswell Publishing
Perth, Western Australia
upswellpublishing.com

ISBN: 978-0-645-53691-1

A catalogue record for this
book is available from the
National Library of Australia

Cover design by Chil3, Fremantle
Typeset in Foundry Origin by Lasertype
Printed by McPherson's Printing Group

Upswell Publishing is assisted by the State of Western Australia
through its funding program for arts and culture.

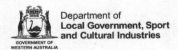

For my daughter, Cecilia

I always thought it would be better to be a fake somebody than a real nobody.

Tom Ripley, *The Talented Mr Ripley*

His stories were good because he imagined them intensely, so intensely that he came to believe them.

Patricia Highsmith, *The Talented Mr Ripley*

The university is a bazaar where a thousand wares are spread haphazardly, while the scholars themselves are turned into peddlers, touts, and pimps, desperately competing to hustle for a few more suckers.

Pierre Ryckmans in his Boyer Lecture, 'The View from the Bridge', 1996.

He had the kind of Scotch-Irish accent which some women find irresistible, and which makes all men feel for their wallet, to make sure it is still there.

James Franklin, *Corrupting the Youth*

OCTOBER 2019, INIS Bó FINNE

On Thursday 31 October 2019, the Irish poet and playwright Tom MacIntyre died at the age of eighty-seven. A memorial tribute published on the same day in *The Irish Times*. There was one glaring factual error: the author described MacIntyre as a 'player of the ancient, fast and furious team game of hurling'. Anyone familiar with MacIntyre would know he was never a hurler. He had played Gaelic football—a very different game—and was a champion goalkeeper in his youth for Cavan, his county, famously saving two penalties in an Ulster championship game against Monaghan in 1958.

The following evening at Day's Bar, the sole pub open during the winter season on the remote island of Inishbofin off the west coast of Ireland, locals perched on stools with their Guinness and Galway Hooker stouts by the open fire. The author of the MacIntyre tribute, a former professor, was flapping his copy of *The Irish Times* above his balding pate, trying to wheedle the uncooperative patrons who were at Day's for a quiet pint into holding a wake for 'the great Irish poet'. He proposed he would read his tribute out aloud, or perhaps even recite a curated collection of MacIntyre's poetry: 'Would anyone care to sing or play an instrument? It will be great craic.'

Billy O'Grady, owner of Wind and Tide, the island's only bookshop, made a quick telephone call to a friend up the road and asked her to come quickly and help evict the drunk professor from the pub. 'Please tell that gobshite to wind his neck in before someone lynches him.'

The friend made her way down to the old quay. 'Get feckin home,' she ordered the professor. 'You're hammered and making a right eejit of yourself in the pub talking shite about wanting to hold a wake for that feckin MacIntyre.'

The raffish Tom MacIntyre arrived on the small island of Inishbofin one spring in the early 1970s. He brought in tow Deborah Tall, a pretty, young American graduate student twenty years his junior whom he had charmed during a short spell as a visiting writer in the English department at the University of Michigan and convinced to move to Ireland to live with him. *I am going to an island off the west coast of Ireland with an Irish writer*, wrote Tall. *The thought still jolts me... Listening to him in class was more like watching a one-man show, the script of which got written on the spot... When I asked him once, on behalf of several friends, if he'd come talk about Yeats some evening at our dorm, he said no, but that he'd talk to me about Yeats one evening over a drink.*

Tall documented their doomed relationship in her memoir, *The Island of the White Cow: Memories of an Irish Island*. An accidental inhabitant, Tall's experience of remote island life was not always a happy one as MacIntyre played out his midlife crisis amidst the backdrop of the Wild Atlantic Way. The islanders had little to do with the couple. Some found MacIntyre aloof and living off their generosity; others felt he was mocking them behind their backs.

MacIntyre and Tall departed after a few short years. Their romantic island idyll shattered. The islanders were not unhappy to see him leave.

OCTOBER 2016, INIS Bó FINNE

Forty-five years later, in early autumn 2016, I set foot on the same Inishbofin pier in a natural and calm sheltered harbour with an Irish professor who had romantically whisked me off to 'his island'. Inishbofin or *Inis Bó Finne* translates from Gaelic as 'Island of the White Cow'. The name is said to have derived from a legend of two fishermen lost in a heavy fog who happened upon an enchanted island. They lit a fire for warmth. Out of nowhere an old woman appeared, driving a white cow along a shingle beach. The woman struck the cow with a stick, and it turned into stone. The woman and the cow are said to return every seven years to warn of impending disaster.

A small, red 75ft steel passenger ferry, the *Island Discovery*, took us from the quaint fishing village of Cleggan a half hour across the glistening North Atlantic to the Island of the White Cow. *All sailing*, announced a sign at the ticket office, *subject to favourable weather conditions*. We took tea before our ferry crossing in the quiet Pier Bar on Cleggan Harbour, the same B&B that had once briefly accommodated Sylvia Plath and Ted Hughes. Plath chose Connemara, with its desolate expanse of mountains, bogs and heathlands, in September 1962 to escape in the destructive year before her death. Confiding that she *desperately needed a boat, the sea, and no squalling babies*, Irish poet Richard Murphy, who hailed from Cleggan, was happy to oblige and brought Plath and Hughes in his sailboat, the *Ave Maria*, a traditional Galway hooker, for a day trip to the Island of the White Cow. During the crossing with a strong current and an ocean swell, Sylvia joyfully leaned out over the prow resembling *a triumphal figurehead, inhaling the sea air ecstatically, as if she were challenging the ocean to rise up and claim her*. The couple spent the day exploring the island by foot, stopping for lunch at Day's pub. Local hotelier and island matriarch Margaret Day later recorded that she liked Sylvia but didn't take to Ted. *He was one person you brought to the island whom I didn't like*, she reprimanded Murphy.

Our ferry was not crowded. Several locals returning home from the mainland with their plastic shopping bags; three amateur cyclists in their neon kits; a toddler swathed in a blue nylon wet-weather suit and a hand-knit brown bonnet balanced on a sea-sprayed step, gripping hard the stair railing as her father stole a sneaky Silk Cut in the stern, blowing the smoke over the bulwark. The crew loaded empty plastic crates stamped *Rose's Superior Salmon Donegal* and *Clogherhead Fishermen's Co-Op County Louth* from the wooden pier and neatly stacked them into containers on deck. The Irish Professor put his back to the mainland and gazed out towards the craggy coastline as we entered the channel of inky water.

JULY 2016, SYDNEY

I had met the Irish Professor in the marbled lobby bar of a Sydney CBD hotel, and he told me, in between countless refills of his glass with a South Australian Shiraz that had stained his lower lip crimson, that he was living 'in exile' in the United Arab Emirates. He spontaneously recited Yeats:

Turning and turning in the widening gyre
The falcon cannot hear the falconer;
Things fall apart; the centre cannot hold;
Mere anarchy is loosed upon the world,
The blood-dimmed tide is loosed, and everywhere
The ceremony of innocence is drowned;
The best lack all conviction, while the worst
Are full of passionate intensity.

The Irish Professor was disarmingly open, articulate and charming. Bespectacled and small in stature, he wore a feminine cashmere Hermès scarf and carried a book, a recent prize winner. His hair, which was cropped close to his scalp, had an unusual shading in three halo rings of colour that gradated in hue from boot-polish black to a steel-wool silver and frost white which made him look like a charming badger. I was captivated and flattered by his attention. He described himself as a 'distinguished professor of ethics' who specialised in 'trust'.

'There can be no doubting the need,' he assured me, 'that the Western liberal order is facing an existential crisis through a calamitous decline in trust. Trust is an essential component of social capital, the glue that facilitates cooperation and coordination for material mutual benefit.'

He recounted a terrible tale of professional and personal misfortune: a recent failed relationship; two disastrous marriages on two different continents; and how he, a loving and devoted father of four, had reported three of his own children from his first marriage to social services in Northern Ireland as he believed his progeny suffering at the hands of a malicious mother and a physically abusive grandfather. 'My first marriage to an Irishwoman worsened through a combination of economic and relational factors. This is not to suggest that economic factors trump emotion factors.' The Irish Professor stared down at his empty glass and paused for dramatic effect, 'It's to say that the subsequent emotional issues as they relate to my children cannot be explained without reference to the impact of the Global Financial Crisis on my former wife's decision to sue for divorce and return to Ireland after a few years in Australia.'

I was momentarily taken aback. I couldn't really see a link between the GFC and the madness and failings he attributed to his first ex-spouse. His eldest son, aged fifteen, was described as 'troubled and troubling' and living by choice in a residential children's care home so that 'he can humiliate his mother and grandfather'. Another child, studying at a university abroad, had ceased speaking to her father since the age of twelve. 'It is of profound sadness that this child has put me in a very difficult moral position, not least because I am a professor with ongoing links to Oxford University.' He explained that she was the beneficiary of a generous scholarship that he believed was not warranted. *You appear to be double dipping*, he wrote to her via his solicitor. *As an adult you must live life as you see fit but I cannot condone the situation. I guess, in part, your complete alienation from me is part of your justification but one cannot have it both ways and, in any event, you should have disclosed this to me and to my lawyer in advance. I am exceptionally disappointed, yours Magwitch*. I pondered his reference to the Dickens character from *Great Expectations*, the former turnip thief Magwitch, driven into a life of criminality and transported to the Antipodes.

Only one child out of the four kept some semblance of contact. The Irish Professor pronounced it fortunate that he had bestowed upon this child his own first name. To distinguish father from son, 'baby' was tacked onto the beginning of his son's name. 'Baby C', he explained to me, was conceived from a terrible argument with his ex-spouse. 'I recall the exact moment of my youngest son's conception. Once the intimate act concluded, my wife gleefully sneered, "Now you are truly trapped!"'

Baby C became the subject of a bitter and protracted custody case across two continents; the other children jettisoned for the favourite. 'I approached the court with clean hands,' he insisted, 'seeking a final resolution to a problem that, despite best endeavours, proved unsolvable. It is all too often that children can and often do become collateral damage as former partners play out past slights and current situations as causally related. I bear my former wife no animosity. I just wanted to protect my children. But I have paid a heavy price to date for doing what I thought was the correct thing to do—reporting disclosures of abuse. I begged social services not to close the file. They did so and unfortunately what happened, to paraphrase Marquez, is a chronicle of an event foretold.'

The Irish Professor's accent was thick, and he spoke so quickly that it was hard at moments to understand what he was saying. He pronounced 'care' as 'curr' and 'cure' as 'corr'. But I fancied his Northern cadence and listening to him animatedly chat. He had a curious way of conversing, as if he were delivering an eloquent and well-rehearsed speech. He recounted being hounded out of Northern Ireland by the IRA; a previous illustrious career as an investigative television journalist; a stint as a popular hotel night-club DJ; a lost year in China; and, most recently, a 'distinguished scholar' who held the record for being awarded multiple research grants at an Australian university. 'For the bulk of my academic career, I have been involved in research-only positions as a consequence of winning competitive grants,' he confided. 'My work is informed by exceptional access to the highest corporate, political and regulatory actors in market conduct and prudential regulation. This allows for an originality in research that attracts significant policy interest and impact.'

I was astonished when he triumphantly asserted that my late father, a respected Sinologist, appeared as a question on his final year East Asian Studies university examination paper. My father had passed away from a brief illness twenty-two months earlier. Grief weighed heavy. The Irish Professor had completed, he said, a BA in politics and obtained a disappointing 2:1. 'But we have much in common, your father and me. I, too, speak Mandarin. Did you ever think he was a spy? I was approached—I should say not unsurprisingly—to be recruited.' He tossed over his right shoulder the luxurious scarf that had loosened, leaned back in the armchair, and winked.

We continued to converse easily about coincidences as hotel patrons entered and departed the busy lobby bar. We had stepped outside into the early-winter evening so he could smoke. He was flatfooted and wore a pair of soft, scuffed, brown leather moccasins that gave him an endearing gait. 'Do you like Paddington Bear?' He showed me a photo from his wallet of a large Paddington Bear he said he'd bought at Paddington Station in London. He stood sentinel in his red plastic Wellington boots, felt floppy hat and navy-blue duffle coat next to a floor-to-ceiling glass picture window in the Irish Professor's apartment in the capital of the emirate of Ajman in the United Arab Emirates. This brief sojourn in the Arabian Desert, he said, appealed to his Jesuit sensibility. 'Paddington is my most prized possession. I take him everywhere with me.'

The Irish Professor tapped out a new cigarette from his pack, pulled a shiny Blackberry out of his suit pocket and proceeded to click through a slideshow of happy snaps of a pretty beach and stone ruin. 'Maggie's Cottage,' he called it. He zoomed in and out with Google Earth. 'It's on Inishbofin, one of the westerly islands off the Irish coastline.' He excitedly explained he was in the process of trying to buy the cottage because Inishbofin was where he had spent blissful summer holidays as a boy. 'You must come with me to my island,' he crooned in his strong Northern accent. A smoke ring floated above his head. 'I have never taken another woman there.'

So here I was. Exact co-ordinates: 53°36.75N and 10°12.45W, seven miles off the rugged Connemara coast on the most western tip of western Europe.

OCTOBER 2016, INIS Bó FINNE

A creaky van drove us up a steep gravel road to the Inishbofin House Hotel, one of only three hotels on the three-and-a-half-mile-long treeless island. After checking in and being introduced to the cheery manager, the Irish Professor insisted we go for a leisurely walk. He wanted to show me the site of the cottage where he intended to build his dream home.

We set off on a long-looped walking track of green roads and single laneways that wrapped round past the ancient stone ruins of St Colman's 14th century abbey before opening to a panoramic vista of the Connemara coastline and Crough Patrick, the famous holy mountain from which St Patrick drove the snakes out of Ireland, visible in the distance. Cue the sudden arrival of flocks of woolly white Shaun the Sheep with little black faces moving slowly in the purple autumn heath on the seaside rocky clifftop and the legendary white cows grazing below in verdant lowland hay meadows. The Irish Professor hummed Van Morrison:

And we'll walk down the avenue again,
And we'll sing all the songs from way back when
And we'll walk down the avenue again
And the healing has begun.

Maggie's Cottage sat on the north side of a horseshoe bay overlooking a tranquil sheltered shale stone beach and towards the sharp peaks of the majestic Twelve Bens of Connemara. We strolled the length of East End Beach wandering between stray strands of seaweed. A lone Ringed Plover circled above and a wooden currach bobbed on its mooring. We reached the stone ruins of the derelict cottage. Half of the slate roof had caved in. Corncrakes nested in the rafters. A side wall had crumbled, giving stray sheep easy access inside. The windowpanes were broken and the wooden door boarded shut. Someone had sprayed graffiti on the back wall. A few metres away towards the seafront, the remnants of another stone wall formed a natural windbreak.

The Irish Professor had been haggling for some time for the property, originally owned by the McHale family, with an islander whose aunt was the eponymous Maggie. It was a tricky negotiation because one first had to be 'accepted' by the small community of one-hundred-and-seventy. They didn't take to outsiders, he explained. There was recognition that friendship and respect had to be earned. But given that he had been coming to the Island of the White Cow 'since a wee lad', the family was prepared to sell him land because 'everything has its price', he proudly declared. 'They call me "the Prof". They trust me.' He slipped his surprisingly small hand into mine and smiled.

The Irish Professor delighted me with the gift of a special seaweed bath at the hotel's Marine Wellness Spa. He said he had business to attend to on the other side of the island and that I should experience the 300-year-old tradition of a nourishing bath with the island's famed algae foraged by locals.

I wandered downstairs and entered a spartan, floor-to-wall white-tiled room with a free-standing bathtub in the middle. Tealight candles strategically placed along the fringe of the dimly lit room faintly flickered. I sank into the salty warm water, squirming to find a comfortable position on the bed of tangled, rubbery kelp commonly known as Bladder Wrack. I willed myself to relax. The promise, according to the spa brochure, was an intensely restorative soak in a *place where time ceases to exist*. I recalled the romantic early-morning walk hand in hand with the Irish Professor along the picturesque East End Beach. I liked hearing him reminisce about his childhood summers on the island and the youthful enchantment of it all. We'd peeled off our rain jackets and he offered to carry mine. I felt a warm contentment and a surprising intimacy.

That evening, we dined in the empty hotel restaurant. Given it was the autumn season on the Island of the White Cow, there were few tourists staying in the hotel and just a solitary waiter quietly drifting.

I selected a home-made creamy seafood chowder. The Irish Professor opted for a roast rack of Connemara Mountain lamb on a bed of Boulangère potatoes. He lit the table candle, leaned forward and caressed my arm. 'Although we are only getting to know each other, I feel I know you implicitly. I can read you because you are open to me, and that is the greatest possible gift you could have given. While it is true that openness can give rise to vulnerability, the trade is worth it.' The waiter placed a small basket of crusty soda bread next to my chowder. 'I have run throughout my life,' he continued. 'The journey was itself the end. For me, the running has ended not through exhaustion but through the tangible reality of achieving inner peace combined with laughter. You are infused with laughter, gaiety and inquisitiveness. What I truly adore about you is the absence of negativity, especially towards others. Being kind is an excellent way to live, and for the very first time in my life, I am living. Living every moment.'

After dinner, the Irish Professor proposed we attend a 'session', an informal gathering of amateur musicians sharing tunes and chat in a pub. It was late, almost midnight, and I was tired, but he maintained that no visit to the Island of the White Cow would be complete without attending or participating in a session. 'It's brilliant craic,' he explained, as we stumbled along an uneven path in the pitch black with just the orange-red tip of his cigarette as a pilot light. 'Musicians, almost like travelling minstrels if you like, voyage from every corner of Ireland to come here and perform all genres of music from classical to jazz, folk and traditional tunes.'

We entered a cosy, low-ceilinged, wood-panelled room. Old photographs and nautical maps were thumbtacked to the walls. He was disappointed that there was not a crowd. Instead, a bored barmaid with dark pencilled-on eyebrows collected empty glasses of Guinness and flotsam of discarded Tayto packets. The Irish Professor ordered a bottle of French Shiraz and said we would need to be patient. 'Someone is bound to sing or play an instrument.' The traditional folk ballad 'Let No Man Steal Your Thyme' drifted from the pub's Spotify playlist, warning young folk of the dangers of taking false lovers:

A woman is a branchy tree
And man's a clinging vine
And from her branches carelessly
He'll take what he can find

An empty bottle of Shiraz later, and when no travelling minstrel showed, the Irish Professor asked the barmaid if she took requests. He asked her to play Van Morrison's 'Into the Mystic'. 'Let's rock her gypsy soul,' he giggled.

The next morning, upon awaking early, the Irish Professor insisted we walk to St Colman's Church adjacent to the mouth of the island harbour to light a candle. Lighting candles, he said, drawing back on a half-lit cigarette, was an important spiritual and symbolic ritual.

We entered the church grounds via a pebble path flanked by two white-grey stone angels kneeling in prayer. Inside the wooden door, a plastic barrel of holy water with spigot sat on a small table covered by a crocheted cloth. The names of island families were commemorated in stained-glass windows: *Pray for the deceased members of our families*, they implored. A memorial window was inscribed to two young American students from Kansas, drowned after being marooned by an incoming tide while out exploring the Stags, an exposed reef with steep columns of rock off the north-west side of the island. A brass plaque was dedicated to those who worked on the re-roofing of the Romanesque cruciform-designed church in 1999.

The Irish Professor genuflected before the altar, took off his glasses and closed his eyes. His lips moved silently in prayer. Outside the church, a cow mooed. The Irish Professor asked if I had a coin to place in the box to pay for two candles—'one for each of us'.

Walking back in a soft rain along the dirt track towards the pier for breakfast, the Irish Professor confided that he was on friendly terms with the Vatican Finance Chief, Cardinal George Pell. Should I wish to seek an annulment for my marriage that had ended a few years earlier, he would be more than pleased to arrange a meeting with the good cardinal to request his services for a decree of nullity, *ab initio*, via an ecclesiastical tribunal.

Many months later, the Irish Professor did buy Maggie's Cottage. He first offered to pay only half the agreed sale price, promising the rest 'soon enough'. The islander, who had a sharp nose for business, wasn't having any of it.

Irvinestown in County Fermanagh, Northern Ireland, in the 1960s when the Irish Professor was born, was a predominantly Catholic rural village. Originally known as Lowtherstown, it was founded in 1618 by Sir Gerard Lowther during the Plantation of Ulster when English King James I flooded Ireland with

English and Scottish settlers. A gifted lawyer and a shrewd politician, Lowther's success was attributed by historians and critics to a 'complete lack of moral principles'.

MJ, known to all as 'Mick', lived with his wife Mary, 'Molly', in a modest two-storey brick home with a dark wooden door on Main Street next door to a small electronics shop selling televisions and radios. A Cork man through and through, Mick migrated to County Fermanagh during the Second World War and from there to Malta before returning to the Lakelands where Molly's family originally hailed.

The O'Reillys had four boys with eighteen years separating the eldest from the youngest. The Irish Professor was the last of the family and only six years old when Desmond and Sons, a clothing manu-facturer, arrived in 1970. Located on the Kesh Road on the site of the old Irvinestown Wanderers football field, the factory produced shirts, tracksuits and pullovers for Marks and Spencer. They were a major employer in the area recruiting local staff. Molly was a manager at the factory and worked hard to support her family since Mick, a former commercial archi-tect, was a heavy drinker and gambled. They did not get involved in the local community and kept to themselves. Molly's only escape was a once-weekly evening game of bridge when Mick was on the bottle.

'It was a deeply unhappy household,' the Irish Pro-fessor confided. Molly, he said, was nothing short of 'a spoilt brat, vain and selfish'. She had trapped his saintly and hard-working father by tricking him into getting her pregnant. He could barely contain his contempt for his mother and was scarred by a particular memory. He had wanted to spend the morning with her, but she was not interested. She declared she was heading out. The Irish Professor did not want her to leave and pleaded with her to stay. She tied on her headscarf and got into the car. As she reversed out the driveway, the Irish Professor clung with both hands to the vehicle doorhandle, stubbornly refusing to let go. His mother accelerated, causing him to stumble and fall hard, scraping his face, hands and knees on the rough asphalt road.

All the stories of his childhood and adolescence centred around the theme of a domestic war that raged inside the home while a civil war raged outside. A bomb scare on his first day of primary school forced an evacuation. Intense sectarianism that he believed reflected deep-seated attitudes honed over generations of 'past slights, insecurities—each self-righteously and proudly displayed'.

To spare her son the misery of home life, Molly sent him in 1976 to high school at St Michael's, a Catholic boys' boarding school sixteen kilometres away in the neighbouring market town of Enniskillen. The Irish Professor worked hard to reinvent himself because he was fearful of being perceived as a 'culchie', a bumpkin from the countryside. He spent his time outside of school at neighbouring houses but never bringing anyone home to his.

He discovered at school that he had a talent for recitation. Naturally confident, he liked being on stage and performing in front of his classmates and teachers. He had an excellent memory and a flair for the theatrical. He won prizes. He explained that like the professional *seanchaí*, the respected traditional storytellers and custodians of poems and folklore who would recite at festive gatherings, it was crucial to have a repertoire because it was a demonstration of scholarship and erudition.

When the Irish Professor was fifteen, Molly passed away from lung cancer. He confessed he 'felt nothing' when the call came through to his boarding school. 'She had already died for me several years earlier.' In 2019, when the eldest brother called to ask for a small contribution to pay for the restoration and cleaning of their mother's gravesite, the Irish Professor bitterly declared to me that he would not donate a cent, such was the hatred he felt towards her. The Irish Professor accused his eldest brother of the lionisation of their mother. 'The past should be left where it belongs in the graveyards,' he vented. 'It is truly time to lay ghosts to rest, and for me Irvinestown is dead.'

Molly and Mick are buried side by side at Sacred Heart Graveyard in Devenish Parish, Irvinestown. On the dark-grey headstone is a simple carved inscription: *Pray for both as you pass by.*

Ten days after our meeting in the hotel lobby, the Irish Professor sent a message from the desert. He announced he was flying to Australia for three days for an important work conference. He asked me to meet him at the airport so he could avail himself of a limousine that was provided by the airline because he always travelled in either Business or First Class. He said he liked the limousine service and derived pleasure from seeing his name and title on a placard held aloft by a chauffeur in the arrival hall.

On the quiet night drive into the city, he murmured that he had absentmindedly left his wallet on the Danish sideboard in his apartment back in the Emirates. Would I mind providing my credit card to reception at the luxury hotel where he was staying, and could I loan him a little money? 'Do not worry, the suite is pre-paid by the university,' he said and patted my arm. It struck me as odd that someone could forget their wallet before flying to another hemisphere. 'I reassure you that I only require the card for incidentals. It is standard hotel policy to present a credit card upon checking in. I shall, of course, reimburse you in full when I next return.'

Upon arrival at the hotel, he greeted the white-gloved doorman in his wool-felt black top hat and burgundy tails with familiarity. 'Shall we adjourn for a quick nightcap before the bar closes?' He steered me towards the lobby bar. 'I have a small confession,' he giggled, and popped a salted cashew into his mouth. 'There is no work conference. I have flown from the

Emirates because I wanted to see you and invite you to dinner. I hope you appreciate the gesture.'

The morning of the Irish Professor's departure, I received an emailed receipt from the hotel. Assuming the hotel had inadvertently charged me for the pre-paid accommodation, I called to clarify the error. I was informed by reception that he had been caught smoking in his suite by a member of the cleaning staff. This automatically incurred a hefty fine. I also noted several bottles of overpriced Shiraz, in-house dining and minibar expenses. Uneasy, I suddenly regretted having offered him my credit card. My stomach churned.

When I messaged the Irish Professor mid-flight in his A380 private First Class suite, he denied that he had, in fact, smoked in the room. He insisted upon his innocence, telling me that hotel staff are notori-ously untrustworthy. 'I would never run the risk of smoking in a hotel room. The cleaning lady is being untruthful.'

Several weeks later, he repaid me the money. As he counted the notes into my hand, he thanked me. 'I know you to be a kind person and I am grateful.' I felt guilty for having doubted his intentions.

OCTOBER 2016, AJMAN

We were sitting in the quiet pool bar of a luxury
five-star hotel in Ajman in the UAE overlooking the
Arabian Sea and a private wide and white beach.
I had flown in at dawn the day before. The Irish
Professor had invited me to spend ten days in the
desert with him. We had known each other only
a few months. I had lowered the drawbridge of my
natural defences. A friend joked that I was a softie
for someone who knew how to spell and punctuate. I
had secretly watched on repeat a brief online video
of a younger Irish Professor giving a university
tutorial on Ireland's state of crisis. I admired how
comfortable and confident he was wisecracking
and performing on stage. I recalled Deborah Tall's
description of watching a one-man show, *the script
of which got written on the spot.*

When I boarded my Emirates flight, an elegant flight
attendant in a stylised red headscarf approached
me with a piece of paper. She asked me my name
and smiled. 'Please come with me to Business Class.
Congratulations on your pending engagement.' I
explained she was confusing me with someone else. I
was not engaged. That said, I was not about to argue
with her regarding a potential upgrade. My phone
suddenly pinged with a message: *Are you surprised?
Do you like your new seat? I hope it is comfortable.* I
quickly messaged back: *Did you arrange this? Why
did she congratulate me on my engagement?* He
responded: *Don't worry, sweetheart. Trust me. It's
common knowledge that if you tell an airline you
are engaged, they will instantly upgrade you. I'm*

a Platinum member so they will treat you well. He attached to his message a YouTube video with instructions: *Press play, lean back and luxuriate in the luxury.* I popped on my headphones and looked through the cabin porthole. A lone baggage handler shovelled suitcases onto a slow-moving conveyer belt into the luggage hold as Van Morrison began to purr:

I want you to put on your pretty summer dress
And we'll walk down the avenue in style
And we'll walk down the avenue and we'll smile
And we'll say 'baby, ain't it all worthwhile?' when
the healing has begun.

The Irish Professor motioned to the bartender at the hotel pool bar to refill our wine glasses. We were the only patrons apart from two men in traditional, spotless white cotton robes and red-chequered head-dresses. He lit a Marlboro and started to talk wistfully again about his youth, ruminating on identity: 'I awoke this morning with an idea of who I am. For me it is the tea. My local hostelry has been serving the same brew for over a hundred years, shipped from Ceylon to Belfast and onwards in tea chests to a hotel in Irvinestown, which on one level is a non-descript country town.' The Irish Professor sucked back hard on his cigarette and absentmindedly tapped the ash down the front of his Canali cotton-twill shirt. 'The ritual is always the same. The leaves can only be stirred in one direction and the preheated pot must be stainless steel. The sight and smell unpack memories of a childhood not idyllic but full of promise. Stir stronger, however, and a much more complex picture emerges of a place that nurtured charlatans and scoundrels, rogues and dreamers, entrepreneurs and hard-working people who navigated their way through the Troubles and beyond, with decency, integrity and not a little wryness... These characters stay with me in my morning ritual, irrespective of where in the globe I happen to be.'

Among the small band of adolescent friends who gathered on weekends was an awkward girl who attended the local Catholic girls' grammar school and who fast latched on to the Irish Professor. She was nicknamed 'the Candlestick' because her nose always ran. Like the character of Pooh Percy (the jealous youngest sister in John Irving's novel *The World According to Garp)*, the Candlestick was unpopular with the others. She harboured romantic feelings for the Irish Professor. The Candlestick, he said, went on to pursue a career in the funeral industry and was his only friend from County Fermanagh.

The subject of being in self-imposed exile was something he kept returning to time and time again. 'The emptiness of belonging, or not, as it happens for me. I guess in the end that is the trade. Opportunity versus stability, certainty versus imaginative exploration. Interpretation of the other—deep, intense and empathetic—over self-reflection. And this is the rub at the heart of the conundrum facing all exiles.' He told me that unless one hailed from rural Northern Ireland, one could not understand the cultural implications and burden. He described what it was like growing up during the Troubles and recounted thrilling stories after graduating from university and of his previous career as a leading television investigative journalist in Belfast and London. Fast-tracked for stardom, he said it all ended when he was forced by the IRA at gunpoint and threatened to never cross the border or risk returning in a body bag: 'My move to the academy was related to the clear and present danger to my life as a consequence of making a series of television documentaries on collusion.'

The Irish Professor's stories were endlessly fascinating to me. I was spellbound. As the sun started to set over the Persian Gulf, he suddenly emptied his glass of Shiraz, butted out his cigarette and spontaneously suggested that we take his Mercedes and drive to Dubai, an hour away on the Emirates Road. The car was permanently parked a few blocks from the hotel in a large, open parking lot. It was coated in thick desert sand as it had not been driven for some months. He paid a youth loitering with a plastic bucket twenty dirhams to quickly handwash it but not before writing our initials within a love heart in the dust coating the windscreen. As an extra treat, he booked a suite at the luxury Westin hotel. We set off on the long desert highway for a night in the wealthiest city of the seven Emirates, the haunting sound of the *adhan*, the Muslim call to prayer, floating from the loudspeakers of a mosque minaret.

Trust is a nebulous concept. At best, it is an abstract mental attitude toward a proposition that someone is reliable, dependable, *trustworthy*. Hemingway suggested that the 'best way to find out if you can trust somebody is to trust them'. The Irish Professor spoke passionately, and often, about his work focused on trust and ethics. *One cannot write about integrity and not live by those measures of probity*, he wrote in a submitted Australia Research Council grant application.

The Irish Professor had gifted me a book, his book: the biography of a disgraced former dean of the Harvard Law School. When presenting me with the slender tome, he told me that he had been a visiting fellow at a prominent centre for ethics at Harvard University and used the opportunity to write the monograph. The Irish Professor described the ambitious dean's glittering career that had collapsed when he was convicted in 1963 for failure to file his income tax returns. This oversight was to cost the dean possible elevation to the Supreme Court, plus prosecution and sentencing to one month's imprisonment commuted to forced hospitalisation and subsequent suspension of ability to practise.

The disgraced dean's portrait does not hang in Harvard's law library, the largest academic law library in the world housed in the modified neoclassical-style Langdell Hall. As The Irish Professor wrote: *Despite the suggestion by Chief Justice Ryan that Landis could once more aspire to greatness, the judge was no doubt aware that the defendant would probably never recover. He never did. A year later he was dead, found floating in his swimming pool three weeks after being suspended from legal practice. The tragedy was complete.*

An Important British Banker was flying to Dubai on a business trip. The Irish Professor decided to hold an impromptu dinner party in his honour with just the three of us. He asked the Important British Banker to bring cheese from London because good cheese was not easy to come by in the UAE.

The Important British Banker arrived with a heavy suitcase. The Irish Professor clapped and laughed when presented with a dozen expensive cheeses. The Important British Banker had brought a sizeable Triple Cream cheese crafted by an artisan producer from Armagh, the ecclesiastical capital of Ireland. This cheese was made from the milk of a single herd of pedigree cows that produced some of the world's creamiest dairy. The Important British Banker, when unwrapping the cheese, reminded the Irish Professor of the time he had extended him an invitation to visit his mystical island of Inishbofin. Travel details and ferry schedules were exchanged. Plans were made for long walks on the Famine Road to Cnoc Mòr in the windswept Westquarter, the Dun More Cliffs and the Children's Burial Ground near Trá Gheal Beach. An avid twitcher, the Important British Banker anticipated a weekend with his binoculars in hopeful spotting of breeding black-backed gulls and Manx shearwaters in the Wild Atlantic Way. The Irish Professor said he would bring a kite that they would fly together.

The Important British Banker duly arrived on the island off the morning ferry after a long trip from London. The Irish Professor was not there to greet him at the Heritage Museum and Souvenir Shop, the designated meeting place. The Important British Banker waited for several hours. There was no reservation made for him at the Inishbofin House Hotel. He took his luggage instead to the family-run Day's Hotel on the waterfront, treated himself to a therapeutic seaweed bath soaking in hand-harvested Atlantic seaweed, wondering where the Irish Professor had vanished.

The dinner party was a big success. 'See?' the Irish Professor said, gently kissing my forehead after farewelling the Important British Banker at midnight, 'We make each other very happy.' I could smell stale tobacco. The Irish Professor told me we were soulmates. 'I am not over-processing, but I have never ever awoken to a Polaroid image of a person. This happened to me three times last week. They are all of you. They are all chaste. And they are all real.' I liked this. I had never known anyone to be so at ease and candid. Although there had not been at first meeting an immediate attraction, the Irish Professor had a romantic intensity that was fast growing on me. My mobile chirruped at all hours, heralding tender text messages. Long, descriptive emails with book extracts, song lyrics and poetry crowded my inbox. I cherished the conversations long into the night.

He spoke of the necessity of rules. These rules, he pronounced, were proof of his commitment. This was reassuring to me. The most important rule was that a soulmate never goes to bed before the other soulmate. This was not good for a relationship. True love, he explained, was retiring to bed together at the same time every night. He repeatedly reminded me that honest communication was essential for a healthy partnership. 'My promise to you,' he whispered late at night when he thought I was asleep, 'is that I shall never lie to you.'

The morning after our successful dinner party, I wandered into his kitchen. There was a mound of melted fromages atop the rustic wooden box from Fortnum and Mason. The Irish Professor had forgotten to put the expensive cheeses into his refrigerator. As I scraped the cream and rinds into the bin, I thought of the white cows grazing peacefully on the enchanted island and recalled the legend of the old woman who had struck a white cow, turning it into stone, and was said to return every seven years to warn of disaster.

The Irish Professor introduced me to a Dutch Businessman, his only friend in the emirate of Ajman. The Dutch Businessman told me he had met the Irish Professor in the bar of the opulent Kempinski hotel where he was having a quiet, after-work cold beer. The air-conditioned bar was a welcome relief from the searing desert heat outside. The Irish Professor had pulled up a chair and offered him a cigarette.

He was talkative. They traded stories, as new friends do, about their professional and personal lives. The Irish Professor told the Dutch Businessman that he had relocated for family reasons to the United Arab Emirates. Introducing himself as a former important television executive and an accomplished academic, he explained he was teaching and researching ethics at a top-rated school of business administration in the Gulf. The geographic position of Dubai allowed for direct connections to Europe, Asia and the Americas. 'While my time here in the Gulf is serving its purpose, it should be considered a career interruption that has temporarily stalled what was a stellar track record in leading, securing and delivering on university research council-funded multi-disciplinary projects on subjects of major policy importance.'

He said he was unhappy living in soulless, cheap university accommodation on campus. Might the Dutch Businessman know of someone who would lease him a luxury apartment opposite the beach? Proximity to water was important to the Irish Professor who fondly remembered a faraway and magical island in the Wild Atlantic off the west coast of Ireland—his Shangri-La. The Dutch Businessman found the Irish Professor lively and entertaining. The Irish Professor recited Yeats:

I will arise and go now, and go to Innisfree,
And a small cabin build there, of clay and wattles
made;
Nine bean-rows will I have there, a hive for the
honey-bee,
And live alone in the bee-loud glade.

The Dutch Businessman confided that he had taken receipt of thirty expensive Persian carpets. They were given to him in lieu of payment from a client who owed him US$25,000 for a job he had done. The Irish Professor was very interested to hear about the Persian carpets and asked if they were of good quality. He proposed that he would assist the Dutch Businessman and sell the carpets for him in Ireland. He said he knew of a reputable antiques expert who was experienced in such matters. The Dutch Businessman drove him to a commercial warehouse in the desert. They carefully unfurled and inspected each Persian carpet before organising delivery of the thirty carpets to the Irish Professor's apartment. He offered to take only a small commission from his Dutch friend for his trouble. The Dutch Businessman shook hands with the Irish Professor to seal the deal. He told me it was because he trusted him.

DECEMBER 2016, SYDNEY

The Irish Professor abruptly left the United Arab Emirates in early December 2016 for reasons I was later informed by the head of department that 'remain a HR matter'. He accepted a position that he and the dean of the Faculty of Business and Economics, a fellow compatriot, had created at a public interest research centre within an Australian university. 'This is how the Irish mafia works,' he explained to me. A research-only position, his brief was to establish a 'centre of excellence' specialising in trust.

His flight was due to land in Melbourne at 10pm on a Sunday. I was delighted that he would be living in the Antipodes. No more long-haul flights across the Indian Ocean and expensive telephone calls from a different time zone. Facebook Messenger, Skype, FaceTime, WhatsApp video and voice calls were all blocked in the UAE and the use of such applications punishable by imprisonment or a fine. The Irish Professor had been able somehow to circumvent the ban, but it was not ideal for communication. He was excited about his return to Australia and talked about 'coming home'. To celebrate, he purchased a Thorens automatic turntable with integrated phono pre-amplifier despite not owning any vinyl, a Paul Smith navy wool-felt fedora and a silver Georg Jensen money box in the shape of an elephant. There was a flurry of romantic text messages sent from the A380 Business Class cabin documenting his journey and a curated playlist of songs. Van Morrison serenaded:

And we'll walk down the avenue again
And we'll sing all the songs from way back when
And we'll walk down the avenue again and the
healing has begun.

It was agreed we would meet the following weekend in Sydney. A reservation had been made for a reunion dinner at his favourite restaurant. His dish of choice was the signature slow-roasted organic lamb shoulder sourced from the chef's own property in the NSW Central Tablelands.

Twenty minutes after his flight landed in Melbourne, my phone lit up with a message expressing disappointment that I was not awaiting him in the arrival hall. Confused, I apologised. This was not what we had agreed. Had I missed something? More messages started popping up, but I couldn't type fast enough to keep up with the barrage. Bewildered by the sudden plummet and change in mood, I tried to call but the Irish Professor cancelled each call, and his phone went straight to voicemail. However, the messages kept coming, increasingly hysterical and accusatory. *This is simply outrageous,* he raged, *you could not be bothered to fly an hour south when I've travelled halfway across the world. I have uprooted my life and my career to return to a continent of philistines who subscribe to a philosophy of 'near enough is good enough'. Clearly, I have made a terrible mistake by returning to Australia. Never speak to me again.*

I frantically pressed redial over and over in a bid to work out what had transpired between the landing gear hitting the runway and his walk-through from customs to the carousel. I sent multiple messages asking him to please call. Silence. He had switched off his phone.

A sleepless night spent anxiously tossing and turning. What had I done wrong? Had I missed a cue? Should I have shirked my work obligations, flown south and bought a welcome balloon? Twelve hours later, a message: *I deeply regret that we fought last night.* Had we fought? I did not recall a fight. I only recalled his outrage. I scrolled back through the correspondence. Another message pinged into my phone: *I was stressed at the thought of returning to the country*

where there are only terrible memories. Please for-
give me.

When the Irish Professor arrived in Sydney the
following weekend, he seemed to have forgotten his
outburst. He urged that we visit St Mary's Cathedral
to light candles. 'I am deeply honoured and proud
you have chosen me. You deserve a life of happi-
ness and laughter and I commit to providing same,'
he whispered, lighting candle after candle in the
semi-darkness beneath the patronal window of Our
Lady, Help of Christians, surrounded by a huddle of
sombre Irish saints.

Strolling late morning through the summer quiet
of the Royal Botanic Gardens, the Irish Professor
announced that he would like to gift me a puppy, specifically a Kerry Blue Terrier. He said he had spoken
with a reputable breeder in Queensland; it would be a
simple process to organise for the puppy to be safely
transported interstate. He recollected his childhood
dog, a Kerry Blue called Charlie. Charlie had been a
faithful companion and his sole confidante 'when a
lonely wee lad'. His older brothers had long fled the
rural village to seek their fortunes offshore, abandon-
ing him to their warring parents. He explained that
the Kerry Blue, although bred to be a working dog,
was reputed for its fierce loyalty. Gifting me a Kerry
Blue would be symbolic of his devotion.

I politely declined his generous gift, citing that my present circumstances not conducive to caring for a pooch. Disappointed, he said this was selfish of me. We continued the rest of our stroll in silence. A trio of white ibis rummaged in an overflowing garbage bin for food scraps left by picnicking tourists.

FEBRUARY 2017, MELBOURNE

The Irish Professor rented a luxury two-bedroom, two-bathroom apartment in a newly opened modern high-rise building with a 24-hour concierge, swimming pool and gym in Melbourne's inner city. His Danish furniture was shipped in containers from the Emirates. Half of it arrived broken and scratched after it was discovered that the local shippers in Ajman had not properly secured everything. Three large Persian carpets were the only relics of his brief spell in the desert. Paddington Bear was undamaged.

One day, strolling in town, he bought an expensive silver flute that he saw in the window of a shop. He had never studied music and couldn't play an instrument. He said he wanted to take lessons. Another time, he returned to his twelfth-floor apartment with an oversized glass terrarium housing a bonsai for his winter garden. A month after his arrival, a top-of-the-range, white Golf GTI with red racing stripes was parked in the garage 'just in case I feel like taking a road trip'. The Bang & Olufsen store two blocks down from his apartment was like a toy shop where he treated himself to the purchase of a large, conical, silver home speaker and a sophisticated music system. Despite outfitting his slick galley kitchen with all new crockery, flatware and matching Le Creuset pots and pans, the Irish Professor never cooked for himself, preferring to take a full breakfast at the neighbouring grand Windsor hotel and dine out each evening in one of the fashionable and popular eateries that flanked his apartment building. Cases of Clonakilla Shiraz Viognier were delivered fortnightly via a local wine merchant.

His usual routine would be to fly to Sydney at the end of each week 'for business meetings'. He always booked a suite at the Westin—the Heritage Wing—for two to three nights. The Irish Professor joked that he should take shares in the hotel chain because he said he had accumulated close to a million points over the years and spent the most time sleeping in their rooms. He even contemplated purchasing the hotel mattress, the Heavenly Bed Mattress and Box Spring, that the Westin offers for sale to its guests in its glossy in-room brochure.

JULY 1960, INIS Bó FINNE

On 25 July 1960, Richard Murphy, the Irish poet who had ferried Ted Hughes and Sylvia Plath across the deep-water channel in his black-sailed Galway hooker, set sail once again from Cleggan pier to the Island of the White Cow. On this occasion, his passengers on board the *Ave Maria* were the celebrated American poet Theodore Roethke and his young model wife, Beatrice.

Roethke and Beatrice lodged at Margaret Day's guesthouse. Their evenings were spent at Margaret's husband, Miko's, pub where it was noted that Roethke thirsted for fame as well as alcohol. Murphy recorded that Roethke was *like a defeated prizefighter, growing bald, groggy and fat* and *dominated the island, and the hotel, with his drinking, bursts of energy, and occasionally, when the fiddle and piano accordion struck up for a dance, he would take off alone around the hall, until he was exhausted.*

Roethke's bouts of heavy drinking and ranting eventually resulted in him menacing the island's matriarch with a large knife. Beatrice and the local doctor signed a certificate of insanity and Roethke was committed to the county asylum in the town of Ballinasloe. Murphy, in his memoir *The Kick*, described Roethke weeping as he *stumbled down the slippery pebbled shore to the wooden punt that was waiting with a man to row him out to the mailboat. The local priest, Fr Mairtin Lang, escorted him on his way.* Murphy was sad to see him go in such circumstances. But Margaret Day remembered *the extreme peace after he'd gone.*

AUGUST 2017, SYDNEY

I was sitting down to lunch on 23 August 2017 with a newspaper editor when the call came through from a Melbourne constable. The Irish Professor had gone missing for three days. His phone rang out. Emails and messages went unanswered. Nobody had seen or heard from him. A colleague had driven to his luxury apartment and pounded on his door. No response. The 24-hour concierge who had a master key explained that, unless the Irish Professor gave permission, he was not permitted by law to enter his apartment. After I pleaded with the concierge that the Irish Professor must have dramatically collapsed on his Persian carpet in cardiac arrest, he agreed to look for him. He went up the lift, rapped loudly on the oak-panelled door, and called out before venturing inside. He described a strange scene: empty bottles upturned on the coffee table and kitchen bench, overflowing ashtrays, dirty clothes strewn over the floor, an unmade bed.

Several hours later, the constable called and reported the Irish Professor had been located. He did not say where. The reason given by the Irish Professor for his mysterious disappearance was that 'he had misplaced his phone and computer chargers'. The constable advised the Irish Professor that in future he should check in with friends and colleagues. The Irish Professor called me not long after and laughingly said, 'You are so sweet to have worried.'

In the European autumn, the Irish Professor returned to the Island of the White Cow. He had finalised the purchase of Maggie's Cottage and wrote to me excitedly to say that a local builder was engaged to commence work and the site was now being cleared in preparation.

He had commenced negotiations with an elderly islander, a widow, to purchase a currach. The widow had put the traditional Irish plank-built boat up for sale after the recent death of her husband. He insisted it did not matter that he had no experience with boats or rowing. He said it would be decorative when upturned and the double gunwale vessel displayed out the front of his new house.

Every evening, he dined either at Day's Bar or Murray's Bar at the Doonmore hotel on the sea clifftop overlooking the harbour entrance, chuntering to the islanders about his important work back in the Antipodes. The Irish Professor waved a fork over a plate of freshly line-caught baked pollock and mash and explained to the fishermen that his job focused on trust and 'banks behaving badly'. The Royal Commission into Misconduct in the Banking, Superannuation and Financial Services Industry was already underway in Australia.

The Irish Professor had been contracted for six months and paid handsomely—$55,000—by the national corporate regulator to appear as an expert witness in a bank bill swap reference rate litigation.

However, he neglected to tell the assembled islanders that a Federal Court judge in his judgement had found the Irish Professor somewhat lacking: *I did not find his evidence as helpful as it should have been*, stated the judge, *and his experience in these areas was significantly less than that of Professor Stultz, whose background I have set out earlier in my reasons and whose evidence I preferred on most but not all of the contested questions... Professor Stultz had more depth of expertise given his extensive background.*

Curiously, when I contacted the corporate regulator four years later in June 2021, they stated that they could not find any record of payment to the Irish Professor. *An initial internal search did not identify him as an expert* was the response from the Professional Standards Unit. The Irish Professor had asked me to witness and sign the final page of his Commonwealth contract, which had also been signed by an authorised delegate, a litigation counsel from the corporate regulator, on 5 September 2017. An internal investigation over several months and subsequent search in the enforcement's team's files eventually revealed that he had been used as an expert and that payment had indeed been made. Ultimately, the Professional Standards Unit confirmed: *an amendment was published on 23 October 2021 to update the details and amount.* The corporate regulator did not wish to broadcast its decade-long involvement and active collaboration in providing support for the Irish Professor's Future Fellowship work, a series of workshops in Sydney, Melbourne, Madrid and Rio de Janeiro moderated by their chairman, as well as multiple Australia Research Council grant applications. One such grant application drafted by the Irish Professor that he had asked me to edit 'for typos' proposed to *advance a national and international agenda on risk culture and misconduct with ASIC making a cash contribution of $50,000 per annum with the research team receiving ongoing access to the Commission and senior executives as required.* Nobody checked if this contribution legitimate. Nor was there any mention of a company established by the Irish Professor that had been deregistered by the corporate regulator when the company's directors notified the corporate regulator they had been signed without their knowledge or consent.

The Irish Professor's passion was his Trust Project. 'What has become increasingly apparent is how the opportunity provided by the end of the Cold War was squandered,' announced the Irish Professor between mouthfuls of pollock washed down with a pint of Connacht Pale Ale. *'Globalization and its Discontents,* the title of Joseph Stiglitz's prescient analysis, has been replaced by a trust deficit, rendered systemically dangerous by the Global Financial Crisis and its aftermath.' The bemused fishermen raised eyebrows, and someone shouted out for another pint.

'I have conceived of the idea of a global exhibition on Trust and its Discontents that will facilitate national and international dialogue and debate. The exhibition is organised in conjunction with Magnum, the most influential photo agency in the world. Its photographers have, over the past seventy years, traversed the globe, bearing witness to pain, isolation, cruelty, hope, faith and cynicism. Its entire archive has been made available to me. The exhibition will open in Melbourne before moving to Singapore, Cape Town, Paris, London, Edinburgh, Dublin, Boston, Santiago and San Francisco, ending up in Paris at the headquarters of the OECD. It will be accompanied by a series of talks, workshops and public lectures bringing together both the photographers and the academy.'

The Irish Professor paused for dramatic effect and lit a cigarette, flicking the ash into the leftover mash. 'But here is my gift to you, the island of 'Bofin and the community at large: I propose to permanently house the exhibition here, upstairs at the Inishbofin House Hotel.'

Murray's Bar fell silent. 'For feck's sake, catch yerself on. What's the big gombeen on about?' asked the local plumber.

MAY 2018, INIS Bó FINNE

In 2018, I chanced upon a message the Irish Professor had sent to a young filmmaker and aspiring actress living in the United States. He had read a short pro-file of her published in *The Irish Times* while eating his hotel breakfast of kippers and buttery scrambled eggs. He very much liked that the filmmaker-actress described herself as a mystical 'seeker'. He found her details on a website and wrote to her.

He told the Seeker that he was a great admirer of her work. He described himself as a 'distinguished scholar' and the director of a ground-breaking global project on Trust; would she consider producing a documentary about him? He believed they were kindred souls. He quoted her Yeats:

I bring you with reverent hands
The books of my numberless dreams,
White woman that passion has worn
As the tide wears the dove-grey sands,
And with heart more old than the horn
That is brimmed from the pale fire of time:
White woman with numberless dreams,
I bring you my passionate rhyme.

When I spoke to the Seeker in March 2022, she said she'd been curious and wished to know more about him and his project. The Irish Professor was enthusiastic in his response: *A major documentary directed by you—a mystical woman of considerable talent—on how my touring exhibition has been constructed, both literally and metaphorically, would be an indication of the depth of talent associated with the exhibition and become a landmark cultural event. More than an exhibit, we are doing a global exhibition as the most ambitious exercise in deliberative governance ever staged. I would like you to explore the world of trust and its discontents. Think world press photo but with the benefit of history. I have exclusive access to Magnum and its photographers. As you are probably aware, it is the most exclusive photo agency in the world. I am interested in how and why trust has been lost. Think using the moving image to explain the still.*

This will not simply win awards—it will change the world. I can meet you in LA or Dublin. I think it is in our mutual and global interests to do so.

The Seeker said that she was charmed by the Irish Professor's eager interest. She 'trusted' the stories he told her. *The documentary is designed for cinematic as well as exhibition release,* he gushed. *I personally like your style. I love people who are inspired and in turn inspiring. I am sure we will get along famously. I look forward to meeting you in person. As a former editor of television current affairs and with twelve years of experience as a documentary filmmaker prior to my academic career, I understand your world. I think we will do a great and worthwhile thing with this project.*

The Irish Professor neglected to tell the Seeker that a news story he had produced for a program he briefly worked on infringed song copyright in both the United States and the UK. The composer, an Irish American rap singer, successfully sued the network. The Irish Professor departed the network not long after the case settled in the composer's favour.

The Seeker explained that, although a bohemian at heart, on a practical level it would be helpful to understand the desired action calendar and delivery date. The Irish Professor wrote to the Seeker: *Let's double the budget and get Barack involved. Not a bad idea,* the Seeker replied. *Do you have a personal contact for Obama?*

The Irish Professor told her he was staying on a magical faraway island—*my island*—in the stormy Atlantic off the west coast of Ireland where he was building a permanent home. He described the rugged beauty of the coastal scenery: *This morning I awoke very early in the dark so I could join the traditional island dawn walk. With each step, I walked towards the light and a horizon of hope. I have never brought another woman to the Island of the White Cow. I should like so much to walk towards the rising light with you. Would you care to come and play with me on my beloved island?*

The Seeker thanked the Irish Professor for such a romantic invitation. She explained that, tragically, her boyfriend's father had been found dead in an apartment in Rio, so the timing was not right. Perhaps at a later time. Disappointed, the Irish Professor responded to the Seeker: *Take your time. Experience your loss. You will, in time, feel better for it (no matter how counterintuitive it seems). As it happens, I have been to Brazil many times and love the soul of Salvador in particular. I will not pry re your boyfriend's father but be there; talk when you are free. All is under control. PS. The definition of commitment is dropping everything to be there in a point of crisis. While we have not met, I adore your empathy. It provides faith that in reaching out we both made the right decision. Be there for your boyfriend and family and when you have time to breathe, I will be here.*

The Irish Professor departed the Inishbofin House Hotel after ten days. He took his Tumi luggage and trundled down to the old pier with a wave and a promise to return in a few months. He left behind a pair of Paul Smith striped pyjamas and a dozen empty wine bottles. The room had to be aired out for ten days and could not be booked as he had defied the no-smoking policy and it reeked of stale tobacco. A bicycle he had hired was found discarded in a bramble thicket. The patient hotel manager who processed his hotel bill, which ran into several thousand dollars, told me later that he paid with the university corporate credit card.

MAY 2018, SYDNEY

The Irish Professor had flown to Sydney on a mild autumn afternoon in 2018 and asked to meet at a popular bar. When I arrived, there was a growing collection of empty wine glasses and discarded cigarette butts. Distracted, unshaven, his Italian suit was crumpled, and I could see a ring of grime around the collar and cuffs of his white Charvet shirt. I looked down and noticed that his trouser fly was undone. Had he flown the entire journey with his pants unzipped? I joked. He scowled. He was furiously tapping out a message on his phone and complained that he was under extreme stress trying to 'organise this fecking consortium of academics which is not unlike herding cats. Nobody understands the importance of my work with the Trust Project and what I am trying to achieve. It is typical collegiate jealousy and what I have faced my entire academic career.'

Later that evening, in a sudden pique of rage, he threw a half-eaten pizza at my kitchen wall. The pizza box followed, narrowly missing my head.

After his return from the Island of the White Cow, the Irish Professor spent weeks sequestered in his Melbourne apartment chain-smoking Marlboro Reds and labouring over complex and detailed applications for important university research grants. He was not required to work in the university office; he preferred to work from his apartment as he did not like the commute. The white Golf GTI sat in his apartment building garage. I imagined, like his Mercedes in Ajman, that it was slowly being cloaked in dust.

The Irish Professor was also extremely busy culling hundreds of Magnum photographs for his travelling trust exhibition. *Congrats to the deal-making dervish!* Crowed one academic to the Irish Professor, *you have done extremely well to pull all this together.*

He had flown First Class to London to meet with the global cultural director of Magnum and on to Dublin where he engaged a leading interpretative design consultancy to commence designing the exhibition proper. The design consultancy was renowned for developing purpose-specific exhibitions, including an award-winning design for the Titanic exhibition in Belfast launched in time for the centenary of the ship's sinking.

The director of the consultancy wrote to me in early 2020 that he'd found the Irish Professor animated, and the concept of a global travelling exhibition on trust fascinating. The director said the Irish Professor reassured him that *the project was live and the money secure.* He requested that a built-in television studio with multiple cameras to allow live streaming and archival recording be incorporated into the exhibition design. The experience, the Irish Professor said, needed to facilitate active engagement. *This is truly a once in a generation opportunity to rebuild trust in distrusting times, thereby serving an essential public good.* The director of the design consultancy had agreed to commence work, he told me, because the Irish Professor 'appeared trustworthy'.

In the early spring of the 1970s, when Deborah Tall arrived on the Island of the White Cow with Tom MacIntyre, there were only 230 people on the island down from 1500 at the turn of the century. The wild Celtic poet and playwright had abandoned his wife and five young children for the romantic reverie of isolated island life and all its attendant creative possibilities at a remove from the commercial world. Tall recalled in her memoir asking MacIntyre: *Wasn't he afraid? 'Fear, child, has no place in the life of an artist.' Was it fair to exact that price from his family? 'There's no fairness in the world,' he said. And he crooned me poetry... And I listened and got looped in the loops of his voice. His enthusiasm was infectious, subversive... I knew I was being talked into*

something, but I liked what he was talking... These are explanations, but the truth is I was bewitched, and my reasoning was vague.

The Irish Professor told me lots of stories. There was the story about his first ex-wife whom he called 'the Soap Monster'. The Soap Monster was a young accountant and daughter of the local vet from a neighbouring village. He brought the Soap Monster and their three young children to Australia because he had taken an important job at a university. The Soap Monster forbade him from entering their home after work via the front door. Instead, he was obligated to go into the garage where there was a large washing machine. He said he was ordered to take off all his clothes and place them inside the machine. Only then was he permitted to enter the house where he would head upstairs and immediately shower. The Soap Monster, he remarked, was frightened he would bring germs into the house.

The Soap Monster liked to spend her days in front of the television tuned in to the home shopping channel. The Irish Professor lamented that she did not cook for him or maintain their household. 'She was like my mother, vain and selfish.' She was miserable living on the other side of the world. She missed her parents. A young niece, one of the daughters of the Irish Professor's second-eldest brother, was conscripted as an au pair to live and work in their rented bungalow. The brother revealed to me one night at dinner that his daughter had told him it was a home heavy with tension and unhappiness. She quickly departed after a few months.

The Irish Professor said that when the Soap Monster asked him for a divorce, 'she did not have to ask twice'. He accompanied the Soap Monster and their children home to their rural village in Northern Ireland. On the long flight, he removed his wedding ring and dramatically flung it across the aisle. It landed in a passenger's pot of yoghurt. He joked that a polite flight attendant brought the yoghurt to his seat, but he told her to 'keep it'.

There was the story about his second ex-wife. He called her the Tyrant. He met the Tyrant early one evening in 2008 at the Westin hotel in Sydney. She was a businesswoman attending a work sales conference gala dinner. He was having a quiet glass of Shiraz in the lobby bar and observing the laughing women sitting in a curved booth. Apparently, the Tyrant's colleague had pointed him out to her: 'Look at that handsome man watching you over there.' The Tyrant looked over his head and asked, 'Where?'

The Irish Professor invited the Tyrant to join him for a drink. He told her he was a global expert in business law and newly separated. 'I love Scrabble, chess, Risk and backgammon. I would love to learn how to play bridge. Can you?'

Recalling to me their first meeting when we met in June 2020 in the southern Sydney beachside suburb where she had lived with the Irish Professor, the

Tyrant disclosed she was entertained by the Irish Professor who spoke quickly and was full of chat. He explained to her that he was on a brief interstate work trip and had packed a kite in his overnight bag. Would she like to come fly his kite with him the following day? Flying kites, he said, was good for the soul. He asked for her number.

The Irish Professor proposed marriage to the Tyrant a few months after they met. He informed her surprised mother that she needed to buy a hat for the occasion.

The Tyrant told me that he took a new job at a new university. This was the third university where he had worked since meeting her. The newlyweds were invited to dinner at the vice-chancellor's harbourside residence. It was a pleasant evening organised to welcome scholars to the academy. On the way home in the taxi, the Irish Professor berated the Tyrant for embarrassing him. He said she was too familiar with the vice-chancellor. It would be preferable, in future, that she stay silent. He told her she was looking overweight.

To celebrate her fortieth birthday, the Tyrant organised a party. She described to me her purchase of an elegant new dress and said she was looking forward to wearing it. The Irish Professor presented her with a cherry-red and mulberry silk qipao mini-dress he had purchased on one of his frequent overseas trips from Shanghai Tang, the luxury Hong Kong fashion house where he liked to shop. The Tyrant was reluctant to wear it. She felt uncomfortable in the fitted silhouette and rigid mandarin collar. She said she looked like a Chinese waitress. The Irish Professor was insistent. 'Trust me. I know what a woman should wear.' Photographs that were taken at her birthday party and posted on her social media show an attractive woman, but her smile is tight.

The Irish Professor frequently travelled. He would fly interstate or overseas. He explained to the Tyrant that his important work as a leading global academic necessitated visiting major cities for high-level discussions with regulatory authorities and leading practitioners from the Monetary Authority of Singapore, the Financial Conduct Authority in the United Kingdom and the International Association of Securities Regulators, as well as its counterpart, the International Council of Securities Associations. He described to her the impressive humidor in the Emirates First Class Lounge cigar bar, with Italian marble, leather couches and custom-built Rolex gold-plated clocks lining the wall. Then he would return to their modest suburban home near the beach with strange, faded bruises. The Irish Professor reassured the Tyrant that his bruises were a result of stumbling in the aeroplane galley during turbulence.

During their short-lived marriage, the Tyrant bought him new teeth. The Irish Professor did not have nice teeth. A study by Queen's University found the Northern Irish have some of the highest levels of tooth decay in Europe. A pan-European survey revealed that Ireland falls below other countries' average when it comes to infrequent tooth-brushing and not regularly visiting the dentist. The Irish

Professor, the Tyrant remarked, was delighted with his new crowns and implants.

There was the story about the Almost Third Wife. The Irish Professor told me he met her in a bar while he was taking a university-funded research trip overseas. He had removed his platinum wedding band which the Tyrant had purchased for him. He asked if he could buy the Almost Third Wife a drink. He told her that he was newly divorced. He spoke earnestly of the importance of 'trust in distrusting times'. He disclosed that prior to joining the academy, he had served with distinction at a media network where he had produced an award-winning news story about Irish conmen selling shoddy mattresses. To expose the chancers, he went undercover. He confessed to the Almost Third Wife that he discovered he had a surprising talent for sales when peddling the cheap pallets to unsuspecting customers. He said he had thrilled at the swindle.

The Almost Third Wife had an important job and she also travelled frequently for work. He bought her a soft cashmere Hermès scarf. He bought one for himself so they could match. He repeatedly told her he felt 'complete. They were complete.' The Almost Third Wife said she never thought of herself as incomplete. When we corresponded in 2021, she shared with me that he gave her the nickname 'Anguille', and quoted her Yeats:

Wine comes in at the mouth
And love comes in at the eye;
That's all we shall know for truth
Before we grow old and die.
I lift the glass to my mouth,
I look at you, and I sigh.

They met up in different cities around the world until the Tyrant discovered his affair. 'Not my finest hour, I must admit,' sighed the Irish Professor. The Tyrant was already aware of another affair with the Filly, an ambitious colleague at the Irish Professor's university and a government-appointed gender advisor to the wrestling federation. The Tyrant told him to leave.

The Irish Professor wrote to an American professor whom he had met at a symposium and explained he needed to get away for a brief spell. The American Professor's Jesuit University in Seattle appealed to his spiritual sensibility and, like St Ignatius, the 16th century mystic and founder of the Jesuits, he said he was embarking on a personal discovery of his own *Consolations and Desolations* as he *walked towards the light.*

After three months in Seattle, the Irish Professor returned home and quickly decamped from his job and second marriage. His colleagues, who rarely saw him as he was always travelling, were informed by the dean that for 'personal reasons' he had to leave. There were stories of a strange flooding in his office, documents destroyed by faulty fire sprinklers. Perhaps a good thing since several hundred thousand dollars of expenses derived from research grants had been clocked up by the Irish Professor on his frequent trips abroad travelling in Business and First Class and staying in five-star luxury hotels with pillow menus. An employee at a competing research centre at the same university was astounded when the Irish Professor submitted a $30,000 bill to her centre and asked for an additional $100,000 to undertake a project at an American university. She recalled rumours of partying on a work trip in Rio where he had gone with a hired crew to film short videos for the university. She said to me that she retained copies of all correspondence for herself as 'an insurance policy in case anything was questioned'. It was a toxic and highly stressful environment, she confided, where academics' egos constantly clashed. The Tyrant had also brought her concerns and evidence of the Irish Professor's extreme expenses to the dean of the law faculty. She said the dean and the university did not wish to comment. They brushed her off.

The Almost Third Wife, he complained to me, was a terrible disappointment because she refused to visit the Island of the White Cow with him. He did not understand why she would not be enchanted by what Deborah Tall described as *a tiny paradise plunked down in the midst of the sea like a gift*. The Almost Third Wife ultimately betrayed him, he said, by her fervent desire to adopt a baby on her own. He had warned her that she would never qualify for the process of adoption without him. 'She went behind my back, was duplicitous and organised paperwork that I refused to sign. I bought her a dog, a Kerry Blue. That should have been enough.'

In late 2016, an Irish constable, Garda Moroney from the Garda Siochána at Clontarf Garda Station, Dublin, made a telephone call to the Inishbofin Island Hotel. He was searching for the Irish Professor who had taken to virtually stalking and harassing the Almost Third Wife. On some days she received twenty messages or more. Over time these messages became increasingly abusive. She had to unplug her home telephone due to repeated calls at 4 and 5am. She blocked contact on whatever platforms she could. He found other means to contact her including e-greeting card services. He sent the Almost Third Wife six abusive emails on 17 June 2016. Garda Moroney, the Almost Third Wife explained to me, had warned the Irish Professor that he had reviewed a file prepared by the Almost Third Wife and her lawyer and was prepared to send it to the Director of Public Prosecutions *with a view to criminal prosecution under Section 10 of the Non-Fatal Offences Against the Person Act 1997*. The Gardaí took the harassment extremely seriously, especially considering its content and persistence. The Irish Professor ceased contacting the Almost Third Wife after his conversation with Garda Moroney.

Two years later, when entering the elegant drawing room at the luxury Merrion hotel in Dublin, the Almost Third Wife saw the Irish Professor taking his tea. When he looked up from the bisque-pink pages of the *Financial Times* and noticed her, she went pale, turned and fled.

The Irish Professor was working very hard on his Trust Project which sought to rebuild public trust and confidence in organisations by *embedding integrity and responsibility.* He was busy writing a book he provisionally titled *Trust and Its Discontents.* He asked me to send early drafts to a dozen publishing houses, but all returned polite rejection letters. By mid-2018, the Irish Professor had established a consortium of four important Australian universities and extracted $100,000 from each for his Trust Project. *The investment demonstrates the esteem in which I am held to steer the agenda and broker a solution,* he vaunted. *It takes a poacher to be a gamekeeper!*

An elderly American District Judge was invited by the Irish Professor to fly from New York to deliver a workshop convened as part of the Trust Project in the offices of a leading global law firm in Melbourne. *I am making plans and weaving agendas!* trumpeted the Irish Professor. The Elderly American District Judge spoke to a small group of businesspeople and academics on 'The Efficacy of Deferred Prosecution'.

A few days after the workshop, the Elderly American District Judge was asked to a private BBQ lunch organised by the Irish Professor at the beachside family home of the Caboose. The Caboose was a close colleague who had worked with the Irish Professor at two previous universities and was responsible for the spit and polish on all the Irish Professor's research grant applications. The Irish Professor told me, 'I have been instrumental in advancing the research career of the Caboose. Under my supervision and mentoring, we have collaborated on a range of initiatives and our close working relationship includes significant publication and grant track records.'

The Caboose was honoured to welcome the Elderly American District Judge to his home. He boasted to me that he had purchased quality pork sausages from a gourmet butcher and juicy wagyu well-marbled rump steaks for the occasion. When the time for the noon BBQ came and went, the Caboose began to fret. He sent multiple messages to the Irish Professor enquiring if there was a problem—had something terrible befallen both en route to lunch? He received no response. He called me late afternoon in Sydney enquiring if I had any knowledge of the Irish Professor's whereabouts. The quality pork sausages, wagyu rumps and potato salad were returned to the refrigerator.

At a little past 5pm, the Irish Professor and the Elderly American District Judge arrived. The Irish Professor was in high spirits and surprised that the Caboose had worried and cleared the table. He joked with the Caboose that it was 'amusing you were concerned'.

On his return flight home to the US, the Elderly American District Judge wrote to the Irish Professor, thanking him for his week in Australia, but requested he please urgently attend to his promise of settling outstanding expenses.

JULY 2016, GALWAY

A Young Consultant holidaying in Ireland for the summer took the Route 20 Bus Éireann from Dublin to Galway via Athlone and Ballinasloe. She chose a window seat towards the middle row. An older man seated in the aisle opposite wearing an extravagant scarf nodded and smiled at her. He leaned across and asked her about the book he had seen her place in her seat pocket. He showed her the book he was reading, a recent prize winner. They chatted easily on their journey towards the gateway to the Wild Atlantic Way. She told him she worked as an independent consultant for an international security firm based in the Middle East. The Irish Professor was delighted. He said he was an expert in 'ethics and security' and was leading a very important global project on 'trust and security'. He asked the Young Consultant if he could enlist her services given their mutual interest. Would she consent to provide him with a full proposal? The Young Consultant, who was well used to working non-billable hours for eager prospective clients, tentatively agreed.

When we spoke in June 2021, she said she was intrigued by the Irish Professor. He excitedly confided that he was building a house on a remote tiny island off the far west coast of County Galway. He was due to overnight in Galway City and had booked a seat on the 923 Citylink from the depot at Foster Street to Cleggan pier to take a ferry to his island. He asked if she enjoyed flying kites. He had packed a colourful kite in the coach's luggage hold. Kite-flying, he said, was good for the soul, as was laughing.

'It is good to laugh.' He showed her a photograph of an oversized Paddington Bear that he said he had bought from Paddington Station in London. He asked if she liked Yeats.

Later that evening, she received a message from the Irish Professor's Blackberry 10 Smartphone: *It was a pleasure meeting with you. If you are still keen, I would love to join you for dinner in Galway tomorrow evening. Remember you are to make the booking! I look forward to swapping stories and of course laughing. Down time is so precious in jobs as demanding as ours are. For now, off to fly my kite and meet with the builder.*

The Young Consultant told me she did not wish to dine with the Irish Professor. Instead, as promised, she sent a draft work proposal in response. She never heard from him again. She said that she did not like Yeats.

APRIL 2018, SOMEWHERE OVER THE ATLANTIC OCEAN, FLIGHT QF 001–SYDNEY–LONDON/EK 415

The Irish Professor was flying constantly interstate and overseas—Sydney, Brisbane, London, Dublin, Cape Town, Mexico, Hong Kong, Singapore, San Francisco and to the Island of the White Cow. He sent a message mid-flight to say that he had success- fully entered into an in-principle agreement with the Organisation for Economic Co-Operation and

Development (OECD) in Paris to use their conference centre to host his global travelling trust photographic exhibition. The City of Light was to be the second-last destination on the landmark exhibition's whistle-stop tour before it was to be permanently housed in the comfortable upstairs reading room and lounge of the popular Inishbofin House Hotel with its peaked gable windows overlooking the Atlantic. He said that it would help boost local tourism to the Island of the White Cow; everyone would marvel at his philanthropic largesse. On a stopover at Changi airport in Singapore, he treated himself to a platinum-coated Mont Blanc pen, Paul Smith wallet and another Hermès scarf. He sent me a selfie, grinning and proudly wearing his new purchase.

On his Emirates flight to the UK, the Irish Professor invited a fellow passenger for a glass of Château Montrose 2005 in the on-board First Class bar. She was an attractive woman who said she worked in the cosmetic industry. They sat together on the plush cream leather settee in the intimate saloon-style bar. She asked him his nationality as she found it difficult to understand him. 'What country do I belong to?' he crooned, as he refilled her glass. 'I hold three passports: British, Irish and Australian. I am culturally Irish, informed by British education and sensibilities, and an Australian attitude to life and its possibilities. As with so many of my peers, I left Ireland in 1983, glad to see the back of it: a civil war in the north; moral, political and economic bankruptcy in the south. No guesses where that brought one? London, then as now, remains the only true global city, where one can forge an identity unshackled from the mores of conservative nationalism.'

The Irish Professor picked at a selection of amuse-bouches, then scooped caviar on a mother-of-pearl spoon onto his fine bone china dessert plate. 'Returning to Belfast and Dublin from 1995–2006 saw a society morph but not change. Sure, we all became richer on paper but what did we do with that wealth other than squander it. And so, Australia and its promise beckoned. After seven years the age-old question: was this an assignment or a home? Uncertain, I moved to Dubai, which has the singular advantage of being the only place in the world where one can travel direct to any other destination. After two years, it was time to move again. The pull was too strong to resist. It means committing to my country and hopefully making it a stronger place.'

He pulled a shiny iPhone out of his Italian suit pocket and proceeded to click through a slideshow of photographs of a pretty shale stone beach, a turquoise-blue horseshoe bay and a half-built house. 'My cottage,' he called it. He zoomed in and out with Google Earth. 'It's on Inishbofin, one of the most westerly islands off the Irish coastline.' The Irish Professor recited Yeats:

Had I the heavens' embroidered cloths,
Enwrought with golden and silver light,
The blue and the dim and the dark cloths
Of night and light and the half light,

I would spread the cloths under your feet:
But I, being poor, have only my dreams;
I have spread my dreams under your feet;
Tread softly because you tread on my dreams.

After disembarking, he messaged her: *Come play with me on my beloved island. I have never taken another woman.* The beautician declined.

MAY 2018, SYDNEY

The Irish Professor invited a former colleague and good friend, the Hyena, to lunch at his favourite restaurant to talk about his Trust Project. The Hyena was a blowsy woman and a professor of pataphysics. Her voice was shrill and loud. He boasted to me when I arrived at the restaurant at the conclusion of their long meal that her successful academic career was owed to her riding in his slipstream at the university where they had once worked together. She blushed. They frequently travelled to international conferences and enjoyed expensive lunches and dinners. I saw her name on most, if not all, of the Irish Professor's drafted and submitted grant applications that he asked me to edit with proposed budgets calculated for travel, accommodation and salaries for *teaching relief and field expenses* topping $1 million: *This investment allows for essential academic research and logistical support.* The Irish Professor ordered a second bottle of the Barossa Felix Shiraz as the

Hyena gossiped about the academy and picked at the carcass of a roast chicken.

'Trust can be defined as having firm belief in the reliability, truth or ability of someone or something,' spouted the Irish Professor, licking his fingers. 'The foundation of trust in the Western liberal state, however, is disintegrating. So, too, is warranted faith in two critical components of institutional trustworthiness: competence and honesty. What, then, as Lenin famously admonished, is to be done?' The Hyena nodded enthusiastically, her freshwater pearls swaying in accord.

When the restaurant started to empty and the patient waiter presented the bill, the Irish Professor paid with his university corporate credit card. He said it was, as always, a very productive work lunch. The Hyena kissed him long and hard on the mouth before tipsily waddling out the door.

A year later, I came across a panicked WhatsApp message from the Irish Professor, telling the Hyena that he urgently needed to *make a quick exit from Australia*. Could she please loan him $15,000 for airfare and other expenses? She immediately, and without question, deposited the money in his offshore bank account.

Expensive custom hi-tech triple-glazed windows and doors had arrived on the Island of the White Cow for the Irish Professor's house. During the winter season construction work had slowed as the gloomy Atlantic weather set in. Asbestos in the old slate roof required specialist removal. The charm of Maggie's original 1930s simple stone cottage was slowly being erased and transforming into a mundane suburban home. Photographs sent by an islander charged with documenting the build showed an unfinished concrete carapace sitting awkwardly and ghostlike, ringed by bundles of rusting wire, discarded plastic pipes and mounds of dumped gravel. The woolly white sheep with black faces had long evacuated and moved to the south side of the pretty horseshoe bay. After many months of awaiting payment, the elderly widow and owner of the wooden currach wrote to explain that she was cancelling the sale. The local builder had sent word requesting payment of his invoices that were now worryingly overdue. The Irish Professor apologised and explained he had been preoccupied with his important Trust Project. He promised that the money would be forthcoming.

14 JUNE 2018, BRISBANE/MELBOURNE

The Irish Professor called from Brisbane airport a little before 12 noon. The university, he revealed, had sent him a letter that he forwarded to me. I read that they had commenced an investigation and given him seven working days to respond to serious allegations of deception and fraud. *For some months, the University has had and has been investigating concerns about your conduct and behaviour in respect of a number of matters. The University now considers that your conduct in relation to the Conduct Issues amounts to serious or wilful misconduct warranting summary termination of your employment under clause 17.2(b) of your Contract of Employment with the University. Before making a decision about this matter, the University wishes to outline the Conduct Issues (and the Allegations comprising the Conduct Issues) to you and give you an opportunity to respond to those issues and the Allegations.*

The conduct issues comprised four allegations including misuse of the university corporate credit card and expenses, bringing the reputation of the university into disrepute as well as allegations of bullying and harassment. Attachments from the faculty finance manager showed almost $100,000 of expenses accumulated in just two months. I recalled the Irish Professor's constant air travel, penchant for fine dining and luxury hotels. Six months earlier, he had insisted on booking a holiday for us at a fashionable resort in tropical far north Queensland. Citing that a week in the sun would 'do him the world of good', he asked for my credit card, explaining that our airline tickets would be purchased via 'points and pay' and the resort accommodation paid with the thousands of points he had worked hard to accumulate. 'This is my gift to you,' he purred.

I subsequently read in the letter of investigation: *In respect of the Sheraton Mirage Port Douglas invoice (Attachment C), which was paid by you using the Corporate Credit Card, you claimed the expense as 'research partnerships'. It was in fact personal expenditure for a private holiday for you (as is clear from the itemised expenses).*

The Irish Professor was outraged. 'I may be many things, but one thing I am most certainly not is a thief,' he vented in between swigs of a Qantas Business Class Lounge McClaren Vale 2018 Shiraz. 'I have never as much as stolen a chocolate bar in my entire life!' He complained he was having difficulty collating receipts to submit to the university. He had already missed two flights back to Melbourne because of the inconvenience and stress brought by the university's letter. He said he would remain in the Brisbane Qantas Business Class Lounge until he could sort through his receipts.

Numb with disbelief, and without telling the Irish Professor, I purchased an airline ticket to Melbourne. I did not wish to let him know that I was en route because I feared another outburst. Nothing made sense.

I arrived at his luxury apartment building before him. The concierge gave me an odd look then quickly cast his eyes downwards and pretended to be busy as I walked through the flashy lobby towards the lifts. Once inside the apartment, I surveyed the scene. Paddington Bear looked grim.

I decided to clean. I hauled the vacuum cleaner from the internal laundry cupboard. A small bundle of clothes—a pair of black skinny jeans with designer rips at the knees and a cheap, clingy red acrylic crop-top—stashed behind the Miele vacuum fell onto the tiled floor. Puzzled, I folded the clothes and placed them by the laundry sink. I started vacuuming the lounge room. The carpet was awash with balls of woolly fluff. I was careful not to suck up the fringes of his expensive Persian carpet or knock over Paddington.

I moved into the Irish Professor's bedroom. The vacuum head struck something hard beneath his Danish King Bo Concept bed. I bent down and scooped up a Lilliputian amber vial no bigger than my little finger. There was a miniature spoon attached to the lid. I carefully washed it out and left it to dry on the kitchen sink.

I was cramming the washing machine with dirty clothes and towels when the front door opened. The Irish Professor walked in. He did not look surprised to see me in his apartment, let alone in a different city. He threw his Paul Smith briefcase on the dining table and shrugged off his suit jacket. 'These allegations are preposterous and unfounded.' He was agitated and began pacing around his lounge room. 'As a pragmatic and professional academic of the highest standing, I recognise that sometimes issues can escalate, especially at times of nervous exhaustion. I am disappointed that these matters could not have been resolved through dialogue but that a fait accompli has been put to me. It is grossly inappropriate for this matter to be judged without cognisance of the facts. This does not demonstrate good faith on the part of the university.' The Irish Professor took a bottle of Clonakilla Shiraz from the kitchen cupboard and poured himself a large glass. 'I believe that matters can and should be dealt with in ways that rebuild trust. Success is determined by trust, appropriately enough, within and between partners.'

On 29 July 2015, an article was published in *The Age* newspaper with the headline: *Walter White approves of this: Ice sales rife on Melbourne's Craigslist*. A Fitzroy North man had been charged with selling ice, or crystal meth, on Craigslist. Advertisements for the drug, codenamed 'puff', 'cold' and 'ice cream', were rampant on the online classifieds site. Craigslist was described as a digital den of iniquity with sex also being sold on the site.

The Irish Professor quickly departed the university. This was his fifth job at a different university in ten years. The expectation was that he would automatically parachute into another institution. However, this time, the ripcord failed.

He despatched an email to colleagues, business associates and friends from the university email address advising of his new contact details. The Irish Professor inadvertently copied in everyone on a group email. He included an unfamiliar name: *Craigslist 6397085223*. When I asked him who and what was *Craigslist 6397085223*, he blanched. I suddenly recalled the small amber vial and the strange clothing. The Irish Professor brushed it off: 'It was nothing. It was a momentary and brief period of madness.

I needed drugs to stay awake as I had important and urgent grant applications to complete. You need to understand that as a former reputable investigative television journalist and documentary filmmaker, I have always had a strong interest in human behaviour and psychology. I invited shemales to partake in drugs—ice and cocaine if you must know—merely to observe them documentary-style. I bought clothing from Target, and I cross-dressed to understand what it would be like to be another person, to truly inhabit someone else's skin altogether. I do not expect you to comprehend, but you must trust me. It only happened on a few occasions.'

The Irish Professor took my telephone and threw it down the toilet. He said he could not risk having any evidence.

JULY 2018, MELBOURNE

The Irish Professor broke the lease on his luxury apartment a week after he negotiated an agreed separation with the university that required him to *resign with immediate effect and that resignation would be accepted by the University.* I read that this was the university's *alternative to finalising further investigation and/or proceeding to termination.* The university concluded that parts of his explanation regarding abuse of the corporate credit card were *highly unsatisfactory* and his conduct alone

constituted wilful misconduct that constituted termi-
nation in accordance with his employment contract.

He forwarded to me a curt two-page letter from
the provost that he demanded I review and edit his
response. When all was officially signed, he sent me
an email on 19 June with just four words: *So it is
done.* Two burly removalists came and packed his
Danish furniture, Persian carpets, Van Morrison CDs,
Hermès scarves and Paddington Bear into cardboard
boxes. Everything was trucked to a storage facility
in the suburbs. Citing that a change of city would do
him good, he took the scenic road trip he had long
promised himself when he first purchased his white
Golf GTI with red racing stripes. He was stopped by a
police patrol car on the Hume Highway near Albury
for speeding and driving an unregistered vehicle with
an expired driver's licence. He charmed the highway
patrolman and escaped with just a heavy infringe-
ment notice for a trifecta of traffic misdemeanors.

He arrived unannounced in Sydney late one afternoon. He asked if he could live in my house 'until
I find a position at a new university'. I recalled the
letter of investigation and agreed separation from
his previous university that he had instructed me
to negotiate and edit. 'Nobody will talk,' he said. 'Let
them think that I have had some kind of a nervous
breakdown.' He was confident that his Trust Project
would be his triumphant calling card at the next
university where he hoped to be employed. As an
early celebration, he gifted himself a giant 55-inch
Bang & Olufsen Beovision television with surround
sound and silver motorised stand. I was deeply

uncomfortable. I reluctantly consented because it was that, he said, or he would drive to The Gap and leap off the ocean cliff into the open Tasman.

SEPTEMBER 2018, SYDNEY

The Irish Professor's days and nights were spent obsessively culling the Magnum photographs for his global travelling Trust Exhibition into five categories of trust: professional, financial, personal, environmental and social. The university, after calling for his resignation, had easily caved in when he requested he be permitted to take the Trust Project with him. They wrote saying they would be prepared to transfer the ownership of any intellectual property created specifically for the Trust Project to another institution and would not seek to restrict him from using the intellectual property. This, despite the university having to settle an outstanding bill from a digital agency that had provided expensive website design for the Trust Project commissioned by the Irish Professor without university approval, as well as repaying significant financial contributions made by several other universities. 'It is a matter of the university safe-guarding its reputation,' a staff member confided to me in 2021. 'Best to quickly exit stage left.'

In a late-night telephone call to the Caboose, I overheard the Irish Professor rehashing the importance of trust and its discontents: 'In an age in which trust is so compromised, with reason, there is neither percentage nor time in failing to address an existential crisis. We need a new form of engagement, a way to communicate that empowers all interested stakeholders. We need to find a way to present the imagery of trust and its discontents.' He showed me a virtual lightbox with over a hundred images. A peppercorn contribution had originally been paid by the university on his behalf, solely for the purposes of research. It provided him with access to the Magnum archives, but he was not permitted to reproduce or commercially disseminate their photographers' works. Magnum trusted him.

I was instructed to collect from a Kwik-e-Print a series of Magnum photographs that the Irish Professor had ordered to be printed and mounted in decorative painted wooden frames. I recognised Steve McCurry's *Afghan Girl*, the arresting portrait of a young refugee child known as 'the First World's Third World Mona Lisa' alongside Cristina de Middel's *Ouidah* and Erich Hartmann's iconic post-war *Empire State Building*. These framed images were a gift from the Irish Professor to himself to *hang on the walls of my island home. I know there are restrictions on use of Afghan Girl but hope we can smooth that over* he reassured the trio of universities that had formed the original consortium for his Trust Project.

Emails from the interpretative design consultancy in Dublin demanding payment for unpaid contracted work for the exhibition went unanswered and ignored. Re-reading the voluminous correspondence from the Irish Professor to the director of the consultancy, I noted that the date of their first meeting in the Dublin studio took place on the anniversary of the sinking of the Titanic.

The builder on the Island of the White Cow was informed by the Irish Professor that he was *very unwell* and that payment—over 100,000 euros— would be forthcoming the following spring. His doctor, he said, advised that it was unwise for the Irish Professor to travel *right at this moment*. Nobody was informed that he no longer worked for the university. New letters of demand arrived weekly and were placed unopened into a shoebox carelessly shoved beneath a couch.

I marvelled at how the Irish Professor had little trouble sleeping. He would doze on my couch with BBC Radio 4's 'Desert Island Discs' playing in the background, snoring in time to the light orchestral valse serenade of the theme music, 'By the Sleepy Lagoon'. Meanwhile, I struggled each night with troubling insomnia and a creeping anxiety. Every time I raised with him that he find alternate accommodation, he would threaten that I would return one day to find him hanging from the rafters of my home.

I received a call late one evening from the Dutch Businessman. He was worried that he had not heard from the Irish Professor in many months. He explained that he had been the person responsible for packing up the Irish Professor's Ajman apartment in December 2016 and supervising the shipping of his belongings to Melbourne. He divulged that there was some money owing to the owner of the luxury beachside apartment. The Dutch Businessman was vexed as he had been the one who helped broker the sublet for the Irish Professor and did not wish to be saddled with his debt.

He recollected a curious incident involving his erstwhile friend who, one evening after drinks with the Dutch Businessman at the Kempinski hotel, messaged him. The Irish Professor told him that upon exiting the luxury hotel, he had been mugged by two young Arabs. He said they took his wallet and made off into the sweltering night. Could the Dutch Businessman please loan him money? The Dutch Businessman returned to the hotel to meet the Irish Professor. He advised that they immediately go to security and pointed out that there were several security cameras strategically placed in the luxury hotel carpark where the Irish Professor said he had been set upon. It would be easy to retrieve the CCTV footage. The Irish Professor refused, saying that it was not urgent and that he would return by himself the next day. In the meantime, he would be very grateful if he could borrow a few dirhams. He promised to repay the Dutch Businessman once the university deposited his salary in his account. Several months later, the Irish Professor asked the Dutch Businessman if the debt could be deducted from the agreed payment he was due to receive once the Persian carpets sold in Ireland. The Dutch Businessman reluctantly agreed.

The Irish Professor pined for his Island of the White Cow. He said his intention was to permanently leave the Antipodes and to end his self-imposed exile. He reminded me that Inishbofin would be built in due course and its construction a form of solace for him. 'The fact I required permission tells you something of my past life. Its characterisation as an escape served only to enrage me. It was my solitary attempt for those around me to understand me.'

He invoked Tom MacIntyre, raging that MacIntyre's genius both as a seer and shaman was destroyed by Deborah Tall. She was a seductive and dangerous vixen, a 'neophyte poetess' who had deliberately betrayed both MacIntyre and the islanders. The Irish Professor was scathing of Tall's memoir which he claimed was vengeful of her mentor, informed by jealousy and rage. Equally, she was resentful of his beloved island 'that gave him what she knew he desired' and of the islanders.

Like MacIntyre, the Irish Professor declared to me that he was on a journey toward authenticity. 'In 1936, having seen his career plummet and his personal life disintegrate, the American writer F. Scott Fitzgerald famously commented that the definition of high intelligence was "the ability to hold two opposing ideas in mind at the same time and still retain the ability to function". It is an aphorism that perfectly encapsulates my position. My island home will provide just that. It will allow for a modest yet creative and productive life... I have reflected deeply, with the help of Aristotle, Seneca and, dare I say it, Nietzsche himself. I return to my island not broken but prepared. The journey to authenticity is a difficult one but it is one in which one needs a compass.'

Unfortunately, this journey could not take him to Ireland via the United Arab Emirates. When he departed the UAE in December 2016, he neglected to repay a bank personal loan. Debt collectors engaged by the bank regularly called and sent angry messages. They had somehow found my contact details. One agent warned me that if he were to briefly transit in Dubai, he would be detained at immigration and risk two years imprisonment.

NOVEMBER 2018, SYDNEY

The Irish Professor revealed one morning that he had nine dollars remaining in his bank account. He was destitute. He sat at my kitchen table with his head in his hands, a cigarette butt smouldering in a full ashtray, the silver Georg Jensen 'Moneyphant' money box tipped on its side and emptied. His eldest brother, who had been financially bailing him out for many years and now diagnosed with Parkinson's disease, called late one night to confide that the Irish Professor had appealed to him for another loan. He implored me to cease giving him money or simply accept that any loans I made to his younger sibling would never be repaid. He revealed that on the last university-funded overseas 'trip', the Irish Professor had impulsively purchased a flashy Range Rover from a second-hand car dealership in Northern Ireland as he did not wish to take, per usual, the bus to his beloved island. He had forfeited the repair warranty if the used-car salesman would agree to knock several thousand euros off the advertised yard price. The Range Rover was driven only twice—from the car dealership in Enniskillen to O. Coyne's carpark adjacent to Cleggan pier in County Galway and back. On the four-hour return trip, a red triangle warning light began to furiously blink on the dashboard. The vehicle was eventually abandoned in the brother's driveway, broken-down, *banjaxed*, and without insurance. The eldest brother was weary. The Irish Professor had angrily written to him. *I am well aware of the chronic nature of your pain and the fact that its constant presence makes it a dull if banal reality with all of the attending enervating mental consequences. I think, however, that you are so caught up in your own travails you fail to see, acknowledge, or have any empathy beyond yourself.*

Previously, I had never pried about the Irish Professor's personal finances. I thought it improper to talk about money. I did occasionally wonder how he managed to maintain such a lavish lifestyle on the modest wage of an academic. I assumed there must have been some kind of inheritance or family fortune. His brother explained that there was an unfortunate history and pattern of excessive spending and living well beyond his means. There was a warehouse, he said, in County Antrim where the Irish Professor had rented a storage unit filled with furniture, Italian suits, electronics and luxury Denby dinnerware. I imagined that there was also a box of plush Paddington Bears in different sizes.

The Irish Professor pawned his expensive telephone and a camera. His silver flute was sold online to an elderly retired music teacher who travelled from the South Coast to collect it. A young couple setting up a new home bought one of the Bang & Olufsen speakers that looked like a satellite dish on walnut- wood legs. The Irish Professor received unemployment benefits. He devised a plan and asked a Clever Psychiatrist to write a medical report in support of an application to his superannuation fund in the UK so he could draw his university pension based on *early retirement due to an incapacity to work.* The Clever Psychiatrist was happy to assist.

The Irish Professor had started seeing the Clever Psychiatrist five days a week. He wrote to me and his brothers claiming, *the psychiatrist, one of Sydney's foremost (allegedly), tells me I need to find a safe place (which of course he charges by the hour for). I am not so sure how helpful this process is going to be; I find myself engaging in playful sparring that reveals as much about him as myself. What is clear, however, is a bold assertion, I make not in pride but in sorrow, it is indeed a curse to be blessed with intelligence bordering on genius.*

I would observe the Irish Professor leaving my house before breakfast, taking books he thought the Clever Psychiatrist would like. The Clever Psychiatrist told me that he enjoyed his intensive sessions with the

Irish Professor, particularly regarding their shared love of literature and Wagner. The Clever Psychiatrist's passion for Wagner's Ring Cycle, *Der Ring des Nibelungen*, featured in an article in *The New York Times* in May 2005: *The Ring seems to be alarmingly popular with psychiatrists (as it is with philosophers, who see Wagner's heroes and gods as embodiments of abstract arguments), though the number of therapists was grossly swollen at Adelaide because the Australian Psychoanalytic Association had scheduled its annual meeting to coincide with the 'Ring.' During the built-in days off, the wine-producing Adelaide Hills were swarming with slurping and spitting Wagner-loving Freudians, Jungians and Kleinians... Also dining at the Grange were three friends in their 40s, often seen at Bayreuth, Berlin, London or Salzburg: Stephen Freiberg, a Sydney psychoanalyst; his partner, Donald Campbell, a designer who successfully markets a silk scarf based on the patterns on the ceiling of the Bayreuth house; and Anne Maree Lucke, a retired schoolteacher from Munich. Together, they make up a fairly representative cross-section of a typical 'Ring' audience.*

JANUARY 2019, SYDNEY

The Irish Professor showed me a letter he had written to the Candlestick in Northern Ireland. His old childhood friend from the village had been in a spot of bother several years earlier after an article published in *The Belfast Telegraph* with the headline:

The disqualified company bosses: Northern Ireland's list of shame. The Candlestick confided to me in 2017 when she briefly holidayed with distant Australian relatives that she was storing a dozen Persian carpets for the Irish Professor. She sent me photographs of the carpets laid out in the rooms of her house. He said she had eagerly entered a sideline business proposed by him two years earlier. It was agreed that they would import and sell luxury Persian carpets in Ireland that the Irish Professor brought back with him on his frequent trips from the United Arab Emirates. He had once trumpeted in a tweet: *Emirates Flight 161! In Dublin with carpets! No Toyota HiAce but carpets at hand for market on Thursday!*

The Candlestick was savvy about selling burial plots but not *au fait* with selling Persian carpets. She had received a response to her request to consign the Persian rugs from a gallery specialising in fine art, sculpture, oriental carpets and textiles housed in a grand Gatehouse in Belfast: *We only deal in specific antique rugs. The Professor's rugs do not fall into a category that would be of interest to our clients.*

The Irish Professor was desperate for the carpets to quickly find homes so he could make some money. He was not happy that the Candlestick, whom he had gifted a cashmere Hermès scarf, was not assisting him as promised. He grumbled: 'She has clearly taken a seat at the cauldron with the other witches in my life.'

Back in the Emirates, the Dutch Businessman had long given up trying to recover his US$25,000 and flying Persian carpets.

MARCH 2019, SYDNEY

The Irish Professor struck upon another idea. Still struggling with unemployment, he decided to apply for paid university PhD programs both in the Antipodes and abroad. He explained to me that it was the best way to ensure some income. His plan was to inform prospective academic supervisors that as an Irishman and a distinguished scholar, he was 'on an eternal quest for knowledge'.

He received multiple rejections until a business school at a university extended him a warm invitation. I read the documents that he shared with me and was astonished that nobody at the university checked if the failed Trust Project, which had been his undoing at his previous university, existed outside of a personal email address. Nobody conferred with any of the six universities where their prospective doctoral candidate had been briefly employed. Nobody asked why a professor already holding an alleged PhD wished to do another.

I reluctantly drove the Irish Professor to his interview at the business school and waited in a nearby cafe. He returned jubilant and declared that an associate professor, 'a woman', was impressed by his resume.

She was honoured to welcome a former distinguished professor to her business school. He told his proposed PhD supervisor that he was the 'director of the Trust Project' and invited her to contribute an article to an important academic journal of which he was general editor (until his sudden departure a few months later after concerns brought by members of the board to the publisher). She was flattered.

The Irish Professor organised a small conference in a boutique inner-city law firm on the forty-first floor with sweeping views of a sparkling Sydney Harbour. I was directed to take photographs of the event. 'Please try and make it look crowded,' he pleaded as I surveyed the half-empty room. He took the pulpit and spoke passionately about *After the Deluge* and the need for responsible conduct of business in the aftermath of the banking Royal Commission. The alleged academic supervisor sat in the front row and applauded loudly. Waiters from the law firm's in-house catering circulated with silver platters of mini croque-monsieurs, seasonal fruit and distributing cocktail napkins. A panel of bedazzled experts at the business school agreed to award the Irish Professor a prestigious government-funded scholarship.

The Irish Professor liked being paid to be a student. The lecturers, he said, enjoyed having a former distinguished scholar in their classroom. The business school engaged him to provide research assistance for discipline experts to progress new units of study proposals in development. He was very pleased to be paid several thousand dollars by the business school to design two units of study, including a very important unit on corporate crime and regulation. A spokesperson from the university explained to me: 'It is common practice for doctoral candidates to be employed to work on projects related to their area of expertise under the supervision of senior academics.'

Meanwhile, I was awoken by telephone calls while emails and text messages continued to ping at all hours from an ambush of debt collectors from the United Arab Emirates trying to recover the bank's unpaid loan and bounced cheques from 'Mr Professor'.

One evening I returned home to find my house unlocked. All the lights were on. The Irish Professor had taken a large, framed sketch off the wall and thrown it on the bed. The sketch, a portrait of me, was a gift from the artist, an ex-boyfriend, who had passed away. The Irish Professor did not like that the painting was in my house. He said it was insulting and hurtful to him. He had covered the painting with yellow sticky notes and scribbled in blue biro, *Sleep with your fucking ghosts.*

I travelled to a work conference interstate. I was looking forward to catching up with friends and colleagues. The Irish Professor asked to accompany me because he did not wish to stay at my home on his own. A welcome dinner had been organised at the hotel. The Irish Professor was seated next to the political editor of an influential newspaper. He told the editor that as a former important investigative journalist, he did not like her newspaper. He said it was an inferior version of its British counterpart. He talked loudly about trust, integrity, and could she please pass him the Lurpak butter to her left? 'Given the calamitous collapse of trust across the Western liberal order, finding mechanisms to address this existential threat is of vital importance,' he assured her. The editor politely smiled, folded her linen napkin and looked away. The Irish Professor buttered his soft dinner roll and continued, 'This is an age in which trust is compromised. One cannot write about integrity and not live by those measures of probity.'

At one in the morning, when everyone else was asleep in their rooms, the Irish Professor shouted at me that I had ignored him at dinner. He launched pillows, a small hard hotel notepad and porcelain saucer at me, and then locked me out of the room.

SEPTEMBER 2019, SYDNEY

The Irish Professor disappeared for four days. When he returned, he said he had holed himself up at the Westin hotel in the city and did not leave his suite. He had run out of money and in-house movies. He went to pawn his Seamaster Omega watch, but it did not fetch the price he wanted. He complained that the pawnbroker could not appreciate a quality timepiece. A week later, he tried to smash a silver clock on my kitchen wall.

JULY 1933, INIS Bó FINNE

On the morning of 8 July 1933, Arthur Kingsley Porter, a Harvard professor, left his stone cottage on a remote island off the coast of Machaire Uí Rabhartaigh, County Donegal, on Ireland's north-western tip, to go hiking. This tiny Gaeltacht island, also called Inishbofin, was overrun with rabbits. He was never seen again.

Porter owned a grand residence, Glenveagh Castle, on the mainland. He had built a two-roomed house on the 120-hectare Inishbofin which he used as a weekender with his wife, Lucy.

The inquest into Porter's disappearance was the first to be held in Ireland without the discovery of a body. The official finding from the investigation was that Porter had accidentally stumbled off a cliff and was washed away by the treacherous Atlantic—death by misadventure. The islanders believed he had faked his own death.

Porter was a troubled man. He was secretly gay at a time when homosexuality was illegal. At the time of his disappearance, he was being treated for depression by the controversial London-based psychologist and physician, Havelock Ellis. Porter's young lover, Alan Campbell, an assistant at Harvard which was a rampantly homophobic institution, had just left him. The Great Depression had begun to drain his finances. Fearful that his double life would be discovered by Harvard University and his career ruined, rumour was that Porter staged his suicide to escape and make a new life for himself. There were unconfirmed sightings of Porter at Parisian nightclubs and a monastery in India; a story of a small fishing boat in the vicinity where Porter allegedly tumbled to his watery grave. In 1933, Porter's disappearance even made the front page of *The New York Times*, a scandalous story that mixed sex, mental health, money and medieval folklore.

A dark stone memorial was erected on the island in 2021 to honour those lost at sea. It does not carry the Harvard professor's name.

NOVEMBER 2019, SYDNEY

The Irish Professor had itchy feet. He wished to travel overseas. Earlier in the year, the Australian government registrar had put in place a Departure Prohibition Order. The Irish Professor, who was required by law to provide for his offspring, had persistently failed to meet his monthly child support payments. He owed the Child Support Agency a substantial debt of accrued fines for non-payment of child maintenance for two of his four children. The

DPO prevented him from leaving the country. He was grounded. When I told him I could no longer afford to loan him money so he could holiday in Shanghai for the new year, he chased me with a filleting knife before tossing it in the sink and threatening, once again, to drive his car to a popular suicide spot on the south head peninsula and throw himself off the ocean cliffs. He momentarily forgot that he no longer owned a car, having sold his white Golf GTI with red racing stripes a week earlier.

DECEMBER 2019, SYDNEY

At noon on 29 December 2019, the Irish Professor presented to a busy police station in Sydney. He was arrested and charged at the counter for a criminal assault occasioning actual bodily harm (AOBH) and malicious damage to property. He was escorted to a grey and windowless back room of the station, interviewed, and his statement taken by a junior constable. He told the constable, 'I may be many things, but one thing I am most certainly not is violent!'

Five hours earlier, as dawn was breaking, I was discharged from hospital emergency. A sympathetic young doctor on the night shift skin-glued a deep gash on my upper lip. 'It's too difficult to stitch.' He apologised, 'I'm sorry, but you will have a small, permanent scar.'

The Irish Professor had attempted to break into my home in the dark. I had told him hours earlier that it was all over. He was incensed. 'You have no right,' he roared. He hurled, with fury, a large teal ceramic garden pot at me. I recalled the sound of rushing air and then standing shocked inside the entrance of my home amid sharp shards of ceramic scattered over the floor, my attacker screaming abuse before fleeing into the night.

Photographs taken by police show my bloodstained white shirt and large splatters of blood on the kitchen counter. One of the ceramic shards had lodged into my top lip like a fish hook. When I drew it out, blood spurted in a perfect small arc and onto the floor. The next day, sweeping the fragments of ceramic into the kitchen bin, I understood that many months of his constant chiselling away had left me broken. I felt the sting of shame. The mounting tension and threat of explosion had had its desired effect. The Irish Professor had foreshadowed weeks earlier that he was like a high-end tourbillon watch: 'simultaneously strong, resilient and exceptionally delicate. Unfortunately the mechanism is hard-wired to detonate at the slightest jolt with huge collateral consequences for which I apologise. Only I know where the wiring goes and only I can disentangle it... I alone am responsible for the mechanism and for what happens when it detonates.'

A month later, an ultrasound and x-ray revealed a three-millimetre tear on my left shoulder rotator cuff where the ceramic pot had struck. A vigilant social worker summoned by the triage nurse interviewed me. Trained to look for marks, she asked about a fading yellowish bruise that ran down my left arm. I did not want to tell her the Irish Professor had crash-tackled me ten days prior and slammed me hard on the cold bathroom tiles trying to wrestle my mobile phone from my hand. Her official report which I later obtained from the hospital concluded that I was *at serious threat.*

Two police officers duly showed up at the hospital, looming large. I was shivering. The friend who drove me to the emergency department pinched a thin cotton blanket left on a stretcher outside the room. The police filmed me with a minuscule camera. They asked me to tilt my head left, right, up, down. They made an audio recording. Took a statement. They told me they were off to arrest and charge the Irish Professor who had fled to an airport hotel. They asked for his photograph to alert the Australian Federal Police at Sydney airport to prevent him from leaving the country.

Weeks following the assault, I found it difficult to focus on anything. In fact, my focus became a lot like the vision test you take for new glasses: head cradled in the shiny machine, staring through a binocular-like apparatus with the optometrist twisting the knobs asking if you can see the clearest letters and images—a little house on a distant hill. But for me, the optometrist had momentarily left the room and everything was fuzzy. I kept wondering when those knobs would turn the right way and the blurriness would clear and events come into focus.

For three months, police reassured me they would secure a criminal conviction. *Based on your admissions and providing a DVEC and visible injuries to police, it constitutes an ABH being intentionally or recklessly with the actions causing bodily harm to the person... Fears held by Police: Defendant will escalate and continue his erratic and aggressive behavior towards others and PINOP* (person in need of protection). They bestowed upon me the label of 'Victim of Crime'.

As I left my home to attend weekly painful physio appointments to repair the tear in my left shoulder, the Irish Professor casually strolled the streets of my neighbourhood and took prime position in my local cafe, the distinctive-coloured *Financial Times* newspaper neatly folded next to his coffee cup. The global pandemic had begun, and the streets were all but deserted. It was the first Sydney lockdown. *I re-read the Albert Camus masterpiece while in Port Douglas,* he posted on LinkedIn, *thanking myself as news reports filtered out from China that I was lucky that I did not travel as planned to Shanghai. Now as the country faces an existential crisis it is time to trust.*

FEBRUARY 2020, SYDNEY

The Irish Professor joined several dating sites. His profile photograph showed him smiling with his new teeth purchased by the Tyrant, wearing a casually knotted crimson Hermès scarf and posing for the camera cradling a large glass terrarium on a city sidewalk.

In March, the same month he was due to face the criminal court for the first mention, a playwright told me that she unwittingly clicked on his profile. The Irish Professor was delighted. He described himself as a poet and a writer hailing from Ireland who was much sought after in the world of international relations. A leading global authority on trust, he said he was the director of Rebuilding Trust, fielding multiple offers of lucrative employment from top-rated universities. Such was his reputation, he explained, that powerful players regularly sought his advice. Because of the pandemic, he was stranded in Australia and living in temporary accommodation at the university.

The Playwright told me she was charmed. She had a deep love of Ireland having visited the country several times. She said she was 'a sucker for a poet' and joked with friends that she would 'one day marry an Irish poet'.

In their first telephone conversation, the Irish Professor proudly spoke of an isolated and mythical island in the squally Atlantic where magical white cows peacefully grazed. The islanders, traditionally suspicious of outsiders, had welcomed him into their small community; they greatly admired and trusted him. Inishbofin appealed to the Playwright's romantic idea of Irish island life. He said he was the proud owner of a beautiful house built out of wood with an expensive stained-glass window, a well-stocked library and two writing studios with large picture windows looking out over a tranquil bay. He promised to take the Playwright to his Island of the White Cow when the pandemic was over so both could write. He serenaded her with Van Morrison's 'Brown Eyed Girl'.

In their second conversation, the Irish Professor told the Playwright that he was close friends with the editor of *The Irish Times*. Would she like for him to organise a meeting with the newspaper's editor to commission articles from her? He also revealed that he was very friendly with the director of a renowned theatre company in Galway and would be happy to assist with staging one of the Playwright's plays. The Irish Professor asked her to send him all her plays for him to read and assess.

Seven days before he was due to appear for sentencing in the criminal court, the Irish Professor wrote to the Playwright: *I heard this, this morning and thought of you* and sent her a poem by Keats:

A thing of beauty is a joy for ever:
Its loveliness increases; it will never
Pass into nothingness; but still will keep
A bower quiet for us, and a sleep
Full of sweet dreams, and health, and quiet breathing.

The Irish Professor told the Playwright many stories. He recounted a terrible tale of personal woe growing up as an only child during the Troubles with a cruel drunkard for a father, and a beautiful and saintly mother. He revered his mother, a deeply spiritual woman, who he said only tolerated his father's merciless taunts for the sake of her one and only beloved son. There was no mention of his three brothers. He said he was blessed himself to have only one precious child, a boy, whom he had named after himself. He missed his son who resided in Northern Ireland with his mother, a harridan who had betrayed him. Disturbingly, the Irish Professor vanished his three other children and a second wife.

The Irish Professor would only call the Playwright late at night. 'No phone call was ever short and sweet—they were three or four hours at midnight where he would just word-vomit,' she said to me. The Irish Professor spoke long and often about Tom MacIntyre and his young lover, Deborah Tall. He affirmed he adored how the pair had romantically run away together to the Island of the White Cow. Above all, he talked about trust and the importance of trust in a relationship. 'You are the kind of woman to fall in love with,' the Irish Professor crooned, 'I believe you may be the love of my life.' Despite his grand and sudden declarations of love, the Playwright felt it was too early to be thinking about committing. After all, they had still not yet met in person.

The Irish Professor went missing for three days. When he reappeared, he explained to the Playwright, who had been concerned by his sudden disappearance, that he had moved out of his temporary university accommodation to care for a close friend, a troubled woman called Prue, who had broken both her arms. 'He complained endlessly about Prue in each subsequent call—how much hard work she was, how he wanted to leave her house, but could not, and how she wanted more with him, but he did not want it. He was quite unkind about her,' the Playwright told me. The conversations that were rich and interesting at the beginning were fast fraying. 'He was obsessed with a $200 wagyu steak from an expensive butcher,' the Playwright recalled. 'He kept asking me if I had ever tasted a $200 steak. He'd been shopping with Prue, and they had bought it together and he had cooked it up and eaten it just before he called me. He went on and on and on about it. He said it was a "sign he was making an impact in the world" and that spending $200 on steak was a status symbol. When I told him that I found it a bit offensive to be talking about $200 steak at a time when people were losing lives and jobs and mental health due to Covid, he spent the rest of the call telling me I was a do-gooder, and it would get me nowhere—that I had to be mercenary and put myself first. I had no issue with the steak, it was his money to spend as he wished, but I took issue with his peacocking about it during such a frightening time in the world's history.'

There was no mention of an apprehended violence order or arrest and charge by the police. There was no indication that the Irish Professor was being hounded by creditors from three different continents, penniless, homeless and a student who was no longer permitted to use the title of professor.

The same story about the fancy *filet* was relayed to me by the cheery manager of the Inishbofin House Hotel. She said she was awoken in the middle of the night by a call from the Irish Professor enthusiastically describing an expensive steak. The first of the Atlantic storms was on its way. The tourist season had finished. Island life was now deathly quiet with long, dark evenings. She wearily replied that she hoped the purchase was worthwhile. He told her he accepted his banishment from the Island of the White Cow. 'I am in exile,' he sorrowfully said.

The Irish Professor was distracted. The days of him disappearing became more frequent. When he did make contact, he would ply the Playwright with questions and demand her fidelity. He talked to her about rules. He was insistent they meet in person and pressured her to do so. Her resistance due to the ongoing pandemic lockdowns made him angry. He commented unkindly about her physical appearance. He said he did not like the look of some of her photos. Had she put on a little weight? 'He seemed to be trying to break down my self-confidence a bit,' the Playwright admitted to me. Her intention was to cease contact with him. However, there was no need as, much to her relief, the Irish Professor suddenly ghosted her. She never heard from him again.

MARCH 2020, SYDNEY

A magistrate finalised an uncontested Apprehended Violence Order for two years against the Irish

Professor under the Crimes Act (Domestic and Personal Violence) three weeks after he criminally assaulted me. He was informed: *Most relationships do not include fear, control or violence. You are now part of a minority of people who has one of these orders, and this is recorded on the NSW Police System.*

On the morning of 4 March 2020, the first mention of the criminal assault occasioning actual bodily harm, the Irish Professor sat quietly flanked by his lawyer in a crowded and brightly lit courtroom on the fifth floor of the Downing Centre Court in Sydney. I observed from my hard plastic seat in the back row that he appeared surprised to find himself in a local criminal court. Small hands folded in his lap. He was not wearing his Italian suit or soft cashmere Hermès scarf. When arrested, the Irish Professor provided a false address to the police and to the court for his bail because he did not wish to alert the university village to his situation. The university had generously provided him with subsidised, comfortable accommodation on campus when he had previously been homeless.

Eight days after the first court mention, two sweaty, panicked policemen pounded on my front door late at night. They said they were searching for the Irish Professor in response to a *concern for welfare job.* The Irish Professor had messaged his ailing eldest sibling in Northern Ireland multiple times. He threatened he was en route to a notorious suicide spot and intended to pitch himself off the sheer cliffs into the swirling Pacific Ocean. The constables mumbled apologies for the disturbance. They explained they had been notified by radio that the 'person at harm' had a recent address listed at my home. Did I perchance have a telephone number for the Irish Professor that I could share with them?

The Irish Professor was eventually found around 3am on campus in his Allen Jack + Cottier award-winning-designed university accommodation and was *spoken to* after police visited several times. Apparently, he was nowhere in the vicinity of the ocean cliffs. According to a friend whom he had called earlier that evening, he had enjoyed a productive and long lunch at the Gaelic Club.

His brother wrote: *Insofar as anyone dealing with the drama, I think we are sadly used to it now.* The second eldest responded: *He is planning a visit to some psychiatric hospital tomorrow. Seems to me that when he sends out a message, he is looking for attention and is enjoying everybody else's discomfiture. Cops have better things to be doing. Enough—a spell in the cold and no further response to self-harm messages. Try watching* Dublin Murders *instead on television!* The constable wearily reported: *After a long conversation, the Irish Professor confessed that he had no intention of self-harming, but said he was just looking for attention.*

I brought this to the attention of the university village and the university. They did not see a problem with law enforcement searching their affordable student housing for the business school's fifty-five-year-old funded doctoral student. Neither did the

Irish Professor's PhD supervisor, the dean of the business school, the vice-chancellor or chancellor.

Many months later, a senior police detective wrote to me: *I have spoken to a DVLO* (specialist officer trained in the dynamics of domestic and family violence procedures). *They are aware of the Irish Professor's history and his vexatious reporting mentality and will liaise directly with me, if need be, should any further incidents arise.*

The Irish Professor, by then, had followed the trade winds and moved north to a rainforest hinterland and a new career as a global DJ with a weekly live world music show on a rural radio station. His personal playlist crossing geographical and genre borders appealed to the manager of the pirate radio station. 'Is it enough to want the beautiful or should you strive for the sublime?' the Irish Professor asked listeners as he cued Van Morrison's seduction dirge, 'And the Healing has Begun'.

APRIL 2020, SYDNEY

On 15 April 2020, the Irish Professor was sentenced pursuant to Section 32. Section 32 of the Mental Health (Forensic Provisions) Act 1990 gives the court the power to divert a defendant into the care and treatment of a mental health professional rather than dealing with them according to the criminal law if they are found guilty of the crime. The Irish Professor was remanded into the care of the Clever Psychiatrist five days a week. This was the same treatment plan he had been following at and prior to the time of the criminal assault. The Clever Psychiatrist wrote a glowing report to the court in support of the Irish Professor. Police advised me that as a 'Victim of Crime', I qualified for a 'Recognition Payment'. This token payment of $1500 would be an acknowledgement from the government that a 'violent crime' had been committed against me. I pondered the reams of paperwork that I was required to fill in and was reminded of the Irish Professor's grant applications. Upon exiting the courtroom, a constable disclosed that had the ceramic garden pot launched by the Irish Professor struck my temple instead of my shoulder and killed me, my family would have received $7500.

The business school at the university rewarded the Irish Professor with ongoing payment for his PhD and a second government-funded scholarship with a substantial tax-free annual income for another three years totalling well over $100,000. Regarding the university's own published code of conduct: *University Expectations of Students: Act honestly and ethically in all dealings with the university and its community*, the response provided to me by the acting vice-chancellor: *As a general matter, please understand that a student's personal history is not a barrier to admission to a degree program.*

Days later, I came across a tweet from one of the associate professors at the business school bleating her support in less than 280 characters for 'female victims of abuse'—by a woman who stayed silent.

Silence, too, from the deputy dean (a woman) and chancellor (a woman). I recalled the 'Aunts', a class of strict, disciplinary women in Margaret Atwood's dystopian novel *The Handmaid's Tale* who work for the Commanders: *The Republic of Gilead, said Aunt Lydia, knows no bounds. Gilead is within you. Doctors lived here once. Lawyers, university professors. There are no lawyers anymore and the university is closed.*

Every academic who was directly involved with either the failed Trust Project or named as a co-collaborator or a researcher in the Irish Professor's multiple drafted and submitted applications for lucrative research grants stayed silent in response to my written inquiries. Similarly, my requests to the business school about its process for vetting scholarship candidates and potential breaches of its own code of conduct resulted in bot-like responses: *Our Student Charter clearly outlines the personal conduct we expect from our students: act honestly and ethically in all dealings with the University and members of its community.* I learned that a curriculum vitae was rarely verified. If somebody had bothered to check, they would have discovered that the Irish Professor was not, as he claimed, an 'honorary professor' at an Irish university school of law or a member of a prestigious English university college, as evidenced in Freedom of Information Requests.

The universities were mute about the glowing letters of support, all self-penned, that were included in his drafted and submitted research grant applications. One such ghost-written letter addressed to the CEO of the Australia Research Council carried the signature of a senior university staffer who later admitted to me that she had not penned the rapturous letter. It did not seem to matter that those other self-penned letters of high praise carried the names of the chair of the national corporate regulator, the governor of the Reserve Bank of Australia and the president of Thomson Reuters. Deloitte, too, remained silent regarding their involvement and claims made by the Irish Professor in clever pitch documents, shared with me, of their global accounting firm committing substantial resources of *1.5 million USD* to his Trust Project. It was catfishing, academic style. *I expect the grants may have caused embarrassment*, confided a former captain of industry, *his misuse of taxpayer funding was extraordinary, as was the alleged cover-up by universities which is why we need a federal Independent Commission Against Corruption (ICAC).* Another finance professional commented: *For my sins of two plus decades in finance, I've seen every conceivable sort of bouncer, cad, sociopath and shapeshifter imaginable. I will have to admit this case is right up there with the most brazen.*

As a former academic wryly said to me, 'If you think the Catholic Church is good at hiding and shuffling priests from parish to parish, just try academia.'

In the early Connemara winter, Matt O'Sullivan Auctioneer, a family-run real estate agency, advertised an island property—ID: MOS-3277—in the shopfront window of its Prussian-blue squat three-storey building in the coastal town of Clifden. An unfinished house was available for sale on the remote island of Inishbofin. It was noted in the advertisement that Inishbofin's *tranquil beauty has over the years magnetically drawn people from various backgrounds. These include artists, poets, writers, and musicians.* The property was listed as under construction and sitting in one of Galway's finest locations. *The current owner wanted to re-imagine history, making a home that retained continuity with the past but ensuring that new technology could be incorporated. In consultation with the architect and Galway County Council an agreed vision was implemented that captures and ignites the imagination. The result is a cottage that seamlessly blends into the landscape but offers a new owner maximum opportunity to stamp their own unique stamp. The home is being offered at this stage so that the final landscaping reflects their own vision... The new owner may wish a traditional or modern approach to interior design and the current builder is happy to install kitchen and sanitary ware of the owner's choice and paint the house at a negotiated fee. The same applies to the choice of gravel or concrete lane way.*

The Irish Professor's half-built house, the original Maggie's Cottage, sold in February 2020 after months of protracted negotiations. A young family from the mainland bought the house with plans to finish it after the wild winter Atlantic storms abated. The local builder was finally paid from the proceeds of the sale after patiently waiting more than eighteen months.

In a long letter to the Clever Psychiatrist, the Irish Professor avowed: *You may recall, I spoke to you in the past about an Irish poet and playwright who lived on Inishbofin and did so to understand not only the Irish psyche but that of himself. In some ways, I am travelling in those footsteps. Whilst it is a journey that has been forced upon me, I also find it one in which I embark upon with a sense of purpose and an ending of a self-imposed exile.*

A few months later, a group of islanders and tourists gathered on a warm summer's evening at Day's Bar on the Inishbofin harbour waterfront dotted with shorebirds, facing the rocky headland and the medieval granite stone ruins of Cromwell's Barracks. This star fort was used in the 16th century to incarcerate Catholic clergy accused of high treason. One unfortunate prelate was allegedly tied to Bishop's Rock at low tide and drowned as the waters rose.

The bar was gearing up for a nightly session of lively traditional Irish music. There was a hog roast—a local pig turning slowly on a spit. It was shaping up to be great *craic*. Van Morrison's ethereal 'Into the Mystic' floated on an overhead speaker:

And when that foghorn blows
I will be coming home
And when the foghorn blows
I want to hear it

The Irish Professor was the talk at Day's. An article had published in an Australian newspaper. It was not authored by the Irish Professor, but instead featured the Irish Professor with the explosive headline: *Trust Project head left university over expense rort.* There was an accompanying photograph of the Irish Professor gesticulating with his small hands. One of the ferry deckhands, a rugged, freckled fellow, reminded the islanders of the autumn evening eight months earlier in late October when the Irish Professor had demanded to hold a wake at Day's for 'the great poet Tom MacIntyre', drunkenly cajoling the islanders to permit him to read out aloud his appreciation of MacIntyre published in *The Irish Times.* 'Sure, he didn't just kiss the Blarney Stone, he slipped the tongue in,' roared the deckhand. A lobster fisherman recalled a comment in response to the disgraced professor's tribute piece. Someone called 'Madashell' had noted in *The Irish Times*: *Hilariously over-written piece (only an academic would produce such pretentious waffle). For example, the phoney drama of the following: 'he boarded a trawler at the fishing port of Cleggan on the west coast of Ireland and sailed into the North Atlantic.' He was sailing to an island a few miles away, for God's sake, not America! Similarly, the stuff about hurling ('the ancient, fast and furious team game'.) Much worse is the laboured attempt to portray MacIntyre's self-imposed isolation on Boffin as some kind of heroic search for authenticity.*

Rubbish. He was an awkward character who found it easier to hide away than interact.

The islanders fell about laughing. Someone knocked over a creamy pint of Guinness at the bar. It shattered onto the wooden floor. 'From rooster to feather duster, ye won't be seeing much of the Prof here anymore!' howled the publican.

Upon departing the Island of the White Cow for good, Deborah Tall wrote: *As I watch the island narrow and fade behind us, I have a terrible dread that I will never see it again... But I know my fear must mean that I've given up the island in my heart. Watching it vanish, that inevitability seems unbearable. There afloat in the channel, the great divide of our lives, I know that this gaunt and gorgeous island has incongruously become a womb, an evasion instead of an outpost. But perhaps, in the end, the island was no escape from reality at all, just a different reality...*

Acknowledgements

My deep gratitude extends to the following people:

Simon Winchester: who encouraged me to write it all down.

My publisher, Terri-ann White, and editor, Nadine Davidoff, for their faith, friendship and unwavering support.

Becky Chilcott, Tara McMahon, Pitch Projects.

Joanna Benjamin, Jo Butler, Helen Garner, Vicki Laveau-Harvie, Amy Richards, Mandy Sayer, Michele Seminara, Anne Summers, Alexa Thomson, Amanda L. Tyler, Justyn Walsh: for generously reading, re-reading and editorial guidance.

Libby Brookes, Anni Gethin, Duncan Graham SC, Jane Hopper, Amy Jones, Detective Joel Loiacono, Gideon Super, Chris Wozniak.

Chris Allen, Tim Ayliffe, Max Bibeau, Gregor Brownlee, Melanie Clulow, Crispin Conroy, Liz Deep-Jones, Jo Dyer, Martin Fahy, Hannah Fink, Hugh Funder, Genevieve Gannon, Julie Hamblin, Sonia Henry, John Hernan, Howard Hilton, Lou Johnson, Dr Karl Kruszelnicki, Martin Krygier,

Peta Levett, Viv McGrath, Carly-Jay Metcalfe,
Rosemarie Milsom, Andrea Morris, Ann Prendergast,
Alison Rooke, Linda Schilling, Guy Schrammel,
Kate Thompson, Eva Timbs, Johnny Timbs,
Viva Vayspap, Michaela Whitbourn, Fionnuala Yau,
Sahar Ghassem Zadeh.

Han Fang, Etienne, Marc, Louis and Alice Ryckmans.

And lastly, in memory of my late father,
Pierre Ryckmans.

References

I have quoted from the following books:

The Talented Mr Ripley (1955) by Patricia
Highsmith; *The View from the Bridge: Aspects of
Culture – the 1996 Boyer Lectures* (1996) by Pierre
Ryckmans; *Corrupting the Youth: A History of
Philosophy in Australia* (2003) by James Franklin;
*The Island of the White Cow: Memories of an Irish
Island* (1987) by Deborah Tall; *The Kick: A Memoir
of the Poet* (2002) by Richard Murphy; *The Collected
Poems of W. B. Yeats* (1906); *The Complete Poems by
John Keats* (1817).

About Upswell

Upswell Publishing was established in
2021 by Terri-ann White as a not-for-profit
press. A perceived gap in the market for
distinctive literary works in fiction, poetry
and narrative non-fiction was the motivation.
In her years as a bookseller, writer and then
publisher, Terri-ann has maintained a watch
on literary books and the way they insinuate
themselves into a cultural space and are
then located within our literary and cultural
inheritance. She is interested in making books
to last: books with the potential to still be
noticed, and noted, after decades and thus
be ripe to influence new literary histories.

About this typeface

Book designer Becky Chilcott chose
Foundry Origin not only as a strong,
carefully considered, and dependable
typeface, but also to honour her late
friend and mentor, type designer Freda
Sack, who oversaw the project. Designed
by Freda's long-standing colleague,
Stuart de Rozario, much like Upswell
Publishing, Foundry Origin was created
out of the desire to say something new.